HARDY ROSES

Hardy Roses

A Practical Guide to Varieties and Techniques

ROBERT OSBORNE

PHOTOGRAPHY BY

BETH POWNING

KEY PORTER BOOKS

Originally published in 1991 by Key Porter Books under the title *Roses for Canadian Gardens: A Practical Guide to Varieties and Techniques*.

Canadian Cataloguing in Publication Data

Osborne, Robert
       Hardy Roses

Rev. ed. of Roses for Canadian Gardens.
Includes bibliographic references and index.
ISBN: 1-55263-307-1

1. Rose culture – Canada.   2. Roses – Varieties. I. Powning, Beth.
II. Title.   III. Title: Roses for Canadian gardens.

SB411.O73 2001   635.9'333734'00971   C00-933224-3

The publisher gratefully acknowledges the support of the Canada Council for the Arts and the Ontario Arts Council for its publishing program.

We acknowledge the financial support of the Government of Canada through the Book Publishing Industry Development Program (BPIDP) for our publishing activities.

Key Porter Books Limited
70 The Esplanade
Toronto, Ontario
Canada M5E 1R2

www.keyporter.com

Cover design: Peter Maher
Electronic formatting: Carolyn Sebestyen

Printed and bound in Canada

01 02 03 04 05 06 6 5 4 3 2 1

For our families,
our friends,
and for the soil
from which all life springs

Contents

Preface

FOR ME, A GARDEN IS A PLACE OF DISCOVERY. EACH TIME I WALK down the paths of my garden, everything is different. The time of year, the time of day, the sun, the clouds, the rain, the fog and the wind—all combine to influence the plants, which themselves are ever-changing. Muted tones of winter flow into the spectral riots of spring and summer and on into earthen fall. The plants grow wider and higher, break and split, flower and fruit. Spiders wait on dew-hung threads to strike, and birds sweep and call. Shafts of light break through the trees, and the patterns dance across the ground.

Gardens are planted and nurtured by our efforts. Our ideas mold gardens into forms, but a humbling magic transforms them into something greater than the sum of their parts and beyond our initial dreams. We create worlds when we create gardens. The planting and cultivating we do initiate cycles of events. A shrub becomes a haven for a bird. The bird eats the caterpillar on the fruit tree. The bird's droppings nourish microorganisms in the soil, and the fine root hairs of a rose absorb the chemical residues left by the decomposing bodies of those organisms and transform them into colorful flowers. Every event triggers other events.

To be a spectator of this fascinating interaction is my greatest reward as a gardener. I revel in the variety of sensations and expectations that a garden offers. The limitless possibilities can overwhelm me as well, and I have to discipline myself to choose avenues of exploration that most appeal to me. After having had countless "favorite" plants, I have abandoned the notion of special status. Each of them is unique and exciting. The rose is not my "favorite" plant, but one that gives me special pleasures and challenges.

Each garden is restricted by its site and climate. You can stretch these limits at times, but not understanding them will lead to failures. My garden is located where winter temperatures can drop to -40°F (-40°C). The firm grip of midwinter can be broken by a mild storm bred in the ocean only to be re-established with intensity as arctic winds push back the warmth. It is a climate that demands endurance and patience both of the gardener and of the plants.

Introducing roses into such a garden seemed a daunting task when I began. The trepidation I felt initially has blossomed into an exhilaration that has me spellbound, not only by the measure of success we have enjoyed but by the sheer variety of color, shape, texture and fragrance that this extraordinary group of plants offers. By accepting the limitations of our cold winters, I was forced to look beyond the more usual offerings of roses—the hybrid teas, the grandifloras, the floribundas—and toward those roses that are less common.

A forsythia blooms in the spring for only a brief but glorious two weeks, yet we treasure it as one of spring's harbingers. Daylilies each last but 24 hours before they are shriveled and done, yet we cannot imagine summer without them. A close examination of a potentilla flower reveals not extravagance but a refined simplicity. Yet, when we see the bush covered with these simple flowers, the effect is overwhelming. We accept these for themselves and find places for them in our gardens. When "shrub roses" are mentioned, though, many gardeners say, "Oh, you mean wild roses" or, "Don't they have only five petals?" If you have passed over the world of hardy shrub roses for these reasons, or if you do not know anything about them, be ready to be enveloped by their beauty and variety.

Any gardener can use and appreciate these roses. Many gardeners see the rose as a symbol of frustration as well as beauty. They may have spent countless hours trying to protect their roses from the ravages of winter, only to be disappointed by failure. Others may have never tried roses because they have heard how difficult they are to grow. This book is an attempt to provide these gardeners with information. Proper nurturing and, more important, proper choice of variety can mean the difference between aggravation and exhilarating success.

It is my desire to convey a heartfelt love of these roses. At the same time, I want to emphasize the need for objectivity in choosing varieties best suited to each gardener's requirements. All these roses are lovely, but all have at least some weaknesses. It is important to define these weaknesses. Therefore I have strived to give a balanced and accurate description of the roses.

Words cannot replace a good picture when it comes to plant descriptions. Beth Powning's photographs are meant to portray each rose's characteristics as accurately as possible. By their artistry, however, the photos transcend this purpose, allowing the viewer to revel in the grace and beauty of each curved petal and the endless shadings of color that make roses so exciting and rewarding to grow.

Special thanks to Freeman Patterson. We would like to acknowledge the help of Sue Hooper, Suzie Verrier, Brian Dykemann and Mike Lowe.

R.O. and B.P.

John Davis, an elegant and hardy rose, is close to everblooming.

PART I

Hardy Roses: The Flowering of a Dream

1

Creating Tapestries

GARDENS ARE AS PERSONAL AS THEIR CREATORS AND ARE AS varied in style, composition and detailing as gardeners are in their hopes, aspirations and temperaments. This is as it should be. One of the greatest joys for any plant lover is to walk through others' gardens. Each garden is unique and conveys something of the creator's dreams and interests. I know of a small perennial garden on a windswept hill. It is tended by a wonderfully selfless and charming gentleman who has devoted his later life to the study of hardy perennials. His garden has no fancy statues, no carefully contoured or planned beds; it simply flows across the landscape as the roots of a plant might work their way through the soil. It is an unassuming, gentle and kindly place. It reflects the very best of this good man.

Although this garden is unstructured, it works. A garden that works, no matter the style, does so because its creator understands the nature of the plants in it. Each plant is unique, having a certain size, color and texture. A creeping phlox grows only a few inches tall; its fine moss-like leaves are a living carpet. In the cool, early weeks of spring, its small, five-petaled blossoms weave their alluring patterns of white, pink, red or blue. The red oak tree, beginning as a lowly acorn, grows to dominate a landscape. Its broad, strong branches thrust out from a massive trunk of deeply furrowed, smoky bark. The leaves, large and pointed, lose their glossy green in autumn, turn to smoldering red, bleach to camel brown, and then hang persistently till the snow's weight or winter's storms scatter them onto the ground.

The simplicity of rose petals scattered across creeping thyme makes a pleasing contrast in textures.

Just as you would never think of using an oak where a phlox would be more appropriate, you should use similar care in choosing material for your garden. Whether you are creating a reproduction of Versailles or an English cottage garden, if you do not have an understanding of your plants' vital statistics, the results will be chaotic and you will be disappointed. With some care and forethought, however, it is easy to create gardens that work without any limitations on your style.

When you are choosing roses for your garden, bear in mind that a rose is not a rose, is not a rose. Roses come in every size, shape, color and texture. For example, Scharlachglut is a vigorous, wide bush with velvety, deep red single blooms that are often as wide as a hand, whereas Double Scotch White is a petite bush with fine foliage and white dainty double blooms a bit larger than a thumbnail. It is difficult to imagine two more different roses. They evoke totally different feelings and have different space requirements, yet each is enchanting. As the gardener, your task is to place these roses in the garden so that each can grow to its potential and at the same time not interfere with either the growth of other plants or the visual arrangement you are constructing.

Hardy roses are a delightfully varied group of plants. Many of them, overshadowed by their aristocratic cousins, were known only to a small group of astute gardeners. As they become more available, and as gardeners' horizons expand, this vast array of plants we group together as "shrub roses" will soon take its rightful place among its peers. Designing with hardy roses is an exciting challenge, one limited only by your space, determination and imagination.

The terminology of hardy roses is confusing. Hardy roses are most often referred to as "shrub roses." The term is also used to mean a rose having a full and generally vigorous appearance. Indeed, I have used "shrub roses" in both contexts in this book. Be warned, however, that not all shrubby roses are hardy and not all hardy roses are shrubby in appearance. To add to the confusion, many people refer to old-fashioned roses as shrubs and others refer to any roses other than hybrid teas or floribundas as shrubs. No one has yet unraveled this maze of definitions to everyone's satisfaction, so in order to avoid total exasperation, let common sense be your guide.

Roses have a rather special place in the history of gardens. More often than not they have been treated somewhat like gems in need of a crown. Many older European gardens devoted a separate section to roses. Often geometric, these rose gardens rarely contained much else in the way of plants. They were designed to dazzle the observer with the shape, color and fragrance exclusively of roses.

In the past century rose growers of the world have fixed most of their attentions on the group known collectively as hybrid teas. Generally speaking, these roses are grown to show off their extravagantly beautiful flowers. The plant itself has been somewhat disregarded or even ignored. As a result, many of these beautiful flowers grow on rather spindly, disease-prone bushes.

The recent revival of interest in shrub or "old-fashioned" roses

Jens Munk, a semi-double rose, is a continuous bloomer.

reflects a changing attitude toward the rose's place in modern gardens. This trend has been convenient for the northern gardener, as many of the hardiest roses belong to several species commonly used before the advent of hybrid teas, floribundas and grandifloras. Because these shrubs have become more popular again, their availability has increased dramatically. The increased interest in shrub roses has also spurred many rose breeders to create shrub roses with longer flowering periods and increased hardiness and disease resistance. The rose garden will never be the same.

More gardeners are integrating the rose into mixtures of plant species. The vigorous *rugosa* roses are becoming backgrounds for perennial borders. Low bedding roses are mixed with low shrubs or annuals. The combinations are endless. The shrub roses, with their solidity and various textures, are choice plants, but the promoter of shrub roses still faces a challenge. The name "rose" has come to be synonymous with hybrid tea and to a lesser extent floribunda and grandiflora. If shown a shrub rose, many gardeners will refuse to acknowledge it as a "real" rose. It does not fit their image of what a rose should be. Because the shrub roses are a fantastically varied group of plants, a great deal of education is necessary to show gardeners how many different uses these plants can have. Once gardeners realize that this wide array of plants offers an exciting challenge to their designing talents, these roses will assume an importance unprecedented in their history.

CLIMBING ROSES

In most cases, climbers are really trailing or pillar roses. They produce long, vigorous shoots that can be tied up. With the exception of a few tender species with hooked thorns, which can work their way up the branches of shrubs or trees, all climbers must be tied to a structure or other plant such as a tree.

One of the more popular uses for climbing roses has been to cover structures such as pergolas, gazebos, trellises and arches. In the past the northern grower has had few hardy climbers to work with. Recently introduced varieties now give northern gardeners the chance to create arches dripping with roses that they could only dream about a few years ago.

Several of these roses owe their existence to the work of two hybridizers – Wilhelm Kordes of Germany and Felicitas Svejda of Canada. Kordes spent a great deal of effort developing roses with disease resistance and hardiness. Some of his releases, such as Leverkusen and Dortmund, combine extreme vigor with a fair degree of hardiness. Working with material developed by Kordes, and crossing it with extremely hardy material, Svejda created a series of long-shooted vigorous pillar roses, which are admirably suited for use as climbers. They are hardier than Kordes's roses but combine many of their best features, such as glossy, disease-resistant foliage and long flowering periods. Some of the best varieties are John Cabot, William Baffin and Henry Kelsey. Another variety worth mentioning was developed by Dr. Walter Van Fleet of the United States at the turn of the century. Using the hardy Prairie Rose (*Rosa setigera*) and the trailing Memorial Rose (*Rosa wichuraiana*), he produced American Pillar, which is still a popular and reasonably hardy climber.

Growing climbing roses requires training. If you leave climbers to fend for themselves you will quickly discover them arching in all directions with little regard for your carefully placed trelliswork. The plant must be tied as it grows, and some pruning is usually called for to keep the rose from becoming too wayward. When tying, use a material that will gradually break down, as ties made of wire will eventually strangle the branches. I have made good use of fence staples when training young roses up a pole or trellis, but the staples must be loosened before they become too tight.

When creating a structure to support climbing roses, the choice of material depends on aesthetics, availability, suitability to the garden and your pocketbook. Brick and stone are premier building materials for durable walls and arches that can create powerful effects in the garden. Gardeners with some time on their hands and a little instruction can create beautiful – and affordable – stone and brick structures. It may take some searching to discover accessible stone sources or a cache of old brick, but the pleasure of creating a structure of brick or stone is hard to match. Wood has been the favored material for most garden structures. It is reasonably easy to work with and generally available. The structure can vary from the most elaborate trelliswork to a simple arch made of rough logs. Although most people are not skilled in iron-

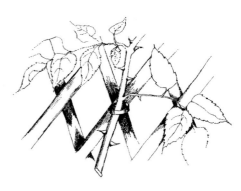

When tying climbing roses to structures, be sure to leave adequate room for future growth. Check the ties annually and loosen them if necessary.

work, beautiful garden structures can be built with this material. A good blacksmith or welder can put together arches or pergolas that can assume a lightness and airiness that belie their strength. I have also seen wonderful arches made with common steel pipe and fittings. No matter which material you choose, only your imagination sets the limits when creating structures for the garden.

A last note concerning climbing roses. Most people associate climbing roses with artificial structures, and of course they are admirably suited to adorn these forms. However, if a suitable shrub or tree is available, there is no better showcase for climbers. Before attaching your rose to a tree, be sure there will be adequate sunshine for your rose and that your tree or shrub will not be adversely affected by its new partner.

SHRUB ROSES

The number of varieties of shrub or bush roses is immense. Most hardy roses fall into this category. They range from rampantly vigorous shrubs 10 ft. (3 m) high to rather diminutive bushes only 3 ft. (1 m) high. Some are very open, while others are very dense.

The most common use of shrub roses is as foundation plants. A shrub rose can be found to fit virtually any space along a house wall. Taller varieties can be used where height is not restricted, and lower varieties can be used under windows. They can be effective when massed together or when mixed with evergreens, flowering shrubs or perennials to create infinite combinations of color and texture.

The rose hedge gives you the chance to use the solidity and vibrant color of shrub roses to full effect. *Rosa rugosa* is perhaps the most important species used in hedging, and for good reason. The dense, rounded form of the *rugosas*, combined with their healthy foliage and tremendous hardiness, makes them very serviceable as well as colorful. Other species can also be effective as hedges. *Rosa alba* and *Rosa gallica* hybrids might be useful where a low informal hedge is desired.

The choice of support structures for climbing roses is limited only by your imagination.

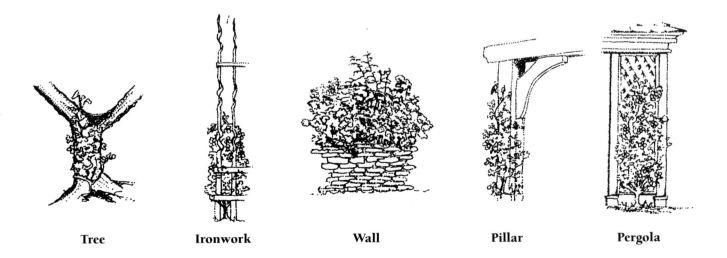

Tree   Ironwork   Wall   Pillar   Pergola

When planted in masses, shrub roses can steal the show from most other plants. The sight of twenty or thirty mature roses in full bloom covering a bed or carpeting a hillside can stir the heart of even a confirmed rhododendron enthusiast. Granted that not every home has the space to house such an extravagance of roses, it is well worth considering when trying to decide how to deal with open spaces. It is important to emphasize maintenance the first few years, but once grown together, a group of shrub roses takes a minimum of care and will repay with an annual display of color that has the power to wash away your burdens and reaffirm to you the gardener the reasons you till the earth.

Shrub roses can, of course, be given their own space in the garden. With a careful arrangement of height, form and color, a spectacular area can be created for roses only. Particularly for the collector of varieties, these "rooms" can provide an area to study, compare and admire. It is worth remembering that if you are planting roses that are not recurrent bloomers, it may be effective to include plants that will be in flower when the roses are not, or perhaps some recurrent varieties of roses, so that that section of the garden is not left colorless for months at a time.

GROUND COVERS

I believe it is fair to say that there are few true ground-cover roses. There are, however, a number of low-growing varieties that can be used to carpet the ground. An example of a ground-hugging variety is the *Rosa rugosa* hybrid Rosa paulii. If grown on its own roots (as opposed to a rootstock), this variety snakes along the ground, never lifting its branches more than a few inches off the soil. It will gradually root into the earth and form a mat, which can be useful to hold steep banks or to form low textural surfaces in much the same manner as creeping junipers. Some trailing varieties can be used as ground covers, though they are not as low and are more cascading.

By using the textures and colors of these lower-growing members of the rose family, you can create exciting visual highlights in your garden. Prostrate varieties can create memorable landscapes when used cascading over a wall or among rocks or specimen plants. Large areas of ground-cover roses, in combination with a high pruned specimen tree or piece of sculpture, can be striking. Low-growing roses placed near water create colorful, patterned edges without making the water seem inaccessible.

A bed of the classic Königin von Dänemark may be used to create an informal look.

2

Wintering

BEAMS OF SUNLIGHT REFLECT OFF THE WARM, PINK PETALS of a rose that is hugging a rocky crag high on a hill in the far north. The steady, cold winds of winter have pressed its red stems against the stones so that they barely rise above them. A month after its fleeting petals are torn away by wind, the first frost coats its leaves. By midwinter the stems are frozen so deeply that a casual touch will shatter them like glass. Yet, under the higher sun of spring, new shoots push from swollen buds, and another year's cycle of growth begins. Farther south, a gardener pokes through her carefully constructed mound of mulch to discover her rose has become a blackened skeleton. All the effort spent in trying to protect the rose from what she imagined was a mild winter has been wasted. How can one rose survive tortuous, frigid winter conditions while the other dies when faced with much warmer winter temperatures? The answer lies in a wondrous process called supercooling.

If you magnified a plant cell, it would resemble a box. The covering of the box is the cell membrane. This rigid structure holds the various fluids and complex structures within its walls, as well as giving the cell its strength. As fall approaches, plants that have the ability to supercool undergo an amazing change. Shorter daylight hours and falling temperatures trigger the cell to reduce the amount of water within it, until all that remains is an extremely thin film of water around the important structures inside the cell. A little-known property of water is its ability to remain elastic well below the freezing point when it is a very thin film. This means that no ice crystals form (ice crystals would rupture and destroy the cell) and the cell can survive extremely low temperatures.

The red rosehips of this hedge provide sparks of color against a wintery backdrop.

Each variety of hardy plant differs in its resistance to ice formation. The hardiest of these plants can survive in a temperature as low as -40°F (-40°C). This is the cutoff temperature for most hardy deciduous plants, although a few evergreens and deciduous plants can actually take all the water within their cells and put it outside the cell wall, in the spaces between the cells. You can find these plants growing well up into the arctic tundra.

Our super-hardy pink rose hugging its cold, rocky bit of earth belongs to those roses that, through countless generations, have developed the ability to use the supercooling process to its maximum limit. The more tender rose has been subjected to temperatures below what it can tolerate, and the expanding ice crystals have quite literally torn its cells apart. It is the challenge of the northern gardener to discover which roses are the masters of supercooling.

A look at the various rose species can be an important aid in deciding which plants will be worth growing in cold climates. In a given species there is usually a good deal of genetic diversity. Plants differ as we do in characteristics. If a rose species is growing in an area where low temperatures occur, those individuals with a greater ability to use the process of supercooling will be more likely to survive, and therefore to pass that ability on to their offspring. This gradual selection process in time allows species to move northward into colder areas. Many rose species, for example, the popular hybrid tea roses, do not have this selection process for cold hardiness. The hybrid teas, although a complex group, were developed from species such as *Rosa chinensis*, which is a native species of southern China. In its native habitat it rarely encounters temperatures very far below the freezing point. Plants of this species have not had to develop the capacity to endure extremes of cold. When growing roses that are derived from species such.as *Rosa chinensis* in gardens with severe winters, the chances for successful overwintering are very poor.

The roses that are successful in northern gardens are derived from species that have been able to adjust to difficult winter conditions through the process of mutation and adaptation. They have become adept at supercooling. Although a large number of species are fairly hardy, only a few have played an important role in the breeding of hardy roses.

The following species of roses form the foundation of most of the hardy varieties in the world. Our best varieties have been selected from these groups. When choosing a rose for your garden, try to find out which species it belongs to. If it comes from one of the following species, it means that it comes from a group with good winter survival skills.

ROSA ALBA

The most expensive perfume in the world pales in comparison to a single bloom from a *Rosa alba*. This ancient species has a special place in rose history and a very precious place in northern gardens. Although little has been done with *Rosa alba* by twentieth-century breeders, the

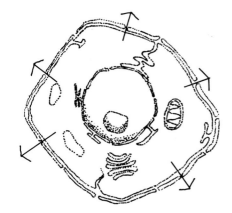

Water being transferred

Supercooled cell

Triggered by the shortening daylight hours and lower temperatures of fall, cells of winter-hardy plants undergo supercooling. Water is transferred outside the cell walls until all that remains is a thin, flexible film of water around the cell's vital components. In this state, the cell can freeze without being ruptured by ice crystals.

older varieties available to us are invaluable. They are generally very healthy, and most are hardy in Zone 4. Some can be grown into Zone 3. Because they do not have a long blooming season they have been relegated to the background of the rose world since the introduction of the perpetual bloomers and the hybrid teas, but I would no more give up my *Rosa albas* than I would my rhododendrons, which bloom for a much briefer time.

ROSA CENTIFOLIA

Peter Beales, in his excellent book *Classic Roses*, tells us that *Rosa centifolia* is not really a species but a complex hybrid comprised of genes from *Rosa gallica*, *Rosa canina*, *Rosa moschata* and others. Be this as it may, the Cabbage rose, as it is known, contains a number of older forms that are both interesting and hardy. Among these are the curious moss roses. These hairy novelties have moss-like glandular bristles that cover the stems and sepals.

ROSA FOETIDA

The double form of this species, Persian Yellow, figures importantly in the breeding of most yellow roses and is the parent of nearly all hardy yellow varieties developed. Considering it is native to southwest Asia, it is an amazingly hardy species, surviving even into Zone 3.

ROSA GALLICA

This species is currently enjoying a resurgence of popularity after having been sadly neglected for nearly a century. Many important varieties were produced in the early and mid-nineteenth century, and these still form the majority of available varieties in the species. However, modern breeders such as David Austin and Peter Beales of England have introduced some stunning new shrub roses with *Rosa gallica* in their blood. Most of the *gallicas* are quite hardy and come in a profusion of colors, including dark tones as in Cardinal de Richelieu, whose flowers are a deep, rich purple. Most have strong perfume, and the flowers are very often double or even quartered.

ROSA RUGOSA

If you had to single out the most important species used in breeding for hardiness, it would have to be *Rosa rugosa*. This native of northern China and Japan has a number of important attributes. Paramount among its virtues is extreme hardiness. Many varieties of *Rosa rugosa* will survive in Zone 2. The flowers of this species are usually large and fragrant, with colors varying from white through the range of pinks to the occasional red. The coarse-textured foliage is unusually healthy.

Blackspot and mildew rarely show up in this species. Lastly, its deep orangey-red hips add a decorative and useful accent to the plant in fall.

My introduction to the world of hardy roses began with the purchase of a Blanc Double de Coubert. Drinking in the sweet, heady fragrance of its first blooms addicted me to roses immediately. This was not a rose that needed to be pampered. It grew defiantly in the garden, scoffing at winter. Ever since discovering this superb ambassador of the *rugosas*, we have concentrated much of our effort on the many excellent hybrids of this species that are now available. If you are living in the very coldest regions, *Rosa rugosa* hybrids are some of the finest and hardiest material.

ROSA SPINOSISSIMA

A species found growing in Europe and Asia, this rose became known as the Scotch Briar rose. It was found in Scotland, and a good deal of selection and breeding work was carried out in the eighteenth and nineteenth centuries in both Scotland and England. From this work arose numerous single and double varieties in whites and pinks. Crossed with Persian Yellow, it gave rise to several yellow forms as well, including Harison's Yellow, the famous "yellow rose of Texas." The small and delicate foliage is unusual. Its thin stems are armed with long, sharp thorns. Generally it flowers once in late spring or early summer, although a few varieties have repeat bloom. One of the better known is Stanwell Perpetual, whose blush pink blooms flower nonstop till frost.

The garden sleeps under its blanket of snow, but its complex pattern of shapes and shadows continues to give pleasure.

3

Nurturing

SUCCESS WITH GROWING ROSES REQUIRES NOT MAGIC BUT knowledge. If you understand the basic needs of your plants and ensure that those needs are satisfied, then the magic that we call growth can take place, and I can think of no more miraculous process than the ability of a plant to suck up water and nutrients, then convert them, with sunlight, into food. In order to make the most of this ability, you need to nurture your roses, to give them all the advantages you can. By providing a healthy soil, adequate water, lots of sun and enough room for growth, you can help your roses reach their potential. Your reward will be the goal of every rose grower – rainbows of sun-washed petals and perfumed evening walks.

SITE

Before you can begin to think about the details of growing roses, you must first decide where you are going to plant them. This can be among your most important decisions. Unless you wish to move, you cannot change your environment. Your position on the globe will determine the general weather conditions and the hours of light available to you. Your particular site will also have a bearing on the garden. Sites differ in soil type, general wind exposure, overall air drainage and, depending upon the size of the site, the alignment toward the sun. Urban environments may affect a site by altering such elements as air quality and light conditions. These are site constraints that you have little control over. Within your site, however, there are often many "microsites." Changing

The soil in which your rose is planted will determine how well your rose grows.

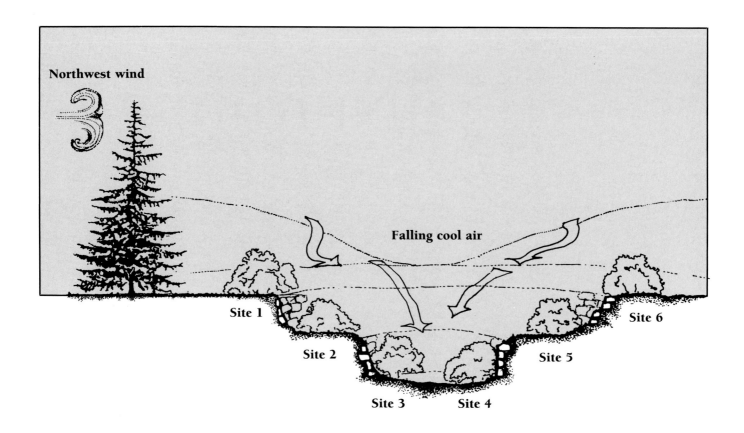

your plant's position within a site, you can often alter the amount and quality of sunlight, the high and low temperatures, the exposure to wind, the water drainage or the soil composition.

When you are deciding where to dig the hole, remember that roses need sunlight. The amount of sunlight will affect plant vigor, flower production and disease susceptibility. The best situation for a rose is full sun from dawn to dusk. Many gardens will not be able to provide this, but try to maximize sun exposure. Roses growing in partial shade will usually be spindly and stingy with their flowers. Roses grown in full shade will slowly die. Sunlight is also an important deterrent to fungal growth. A good dose of sun is far more effective for prevention of mildew or rust than any amount of sprays.

Although we think of ourselves as living in a particular hardiness zone (see the zone map), many sites may contain several microsites that may differ as much as a full zone. The choice of a microsite can greatly affect winter survival. For example, a grove of trees will block the prevailing wind. In winter, a rose planted with this protection would suffer far less from cold, dry winds. These winds can injure a plant by dehydrating it even though the temperature may not be that low. A change in elevation can also be important. On those cold, still nights in spring or fall, frost will form in low pockets where the heavier cold air settles. Higher areas will not be as cold and may escape the frost.

By carefully siting your roses, you can avoid low areas where cold air settles and frosts are more severe. Choose microsites that have protection from high winds, which can lower temperatures and dry plants in both winter and summer. On a typical late spring night, site 1 might be 40°F (5°C), site 2 35°F (1°C) and site 3 below freezing. On a windy winter day, sites 1-4 might be relatively protected while site 5, and especially site 6, may be subjected to severe windchill and desiccation.

Likewise, soil conditions can differ drastically between microsites. Roses are particularly sensitive to wet soils. If their roots sit in water for any length of time, the roots will die from decreased oxygen. In winter, wet soils are colder. Even though the roots have enough oxygen to survive, low temperatures in winter may spell disaster. It is essential that your site be well drained. If you must plant in a wet area, install drain tile to direct water away from the plants. Filling the bottom of a hole with gravel does not solve a drainage problem. If there is no way for the water to escape, the gravel will fill up with water and your rose will suffer as much damage as if there had been no gravel.

The texture and richness of soils will often vary dramatically, even in a fairly small area. If possible, choose an area with a deep, rich topsoil. If there is no such spot, or if your choice of site is guided by other limits, do not despair. Soil is something you can work with to improve.

SOIL

Plants use the soil for anchorage and for sustenance. The soil in which your rose is planted will, in large measure, determine how well your rose grows. A basic understanding of how soil works is essential in managing your garden. Soil is not simply a medium to pour bags of fertilizer on. Rather, soils are complex, dynamic, living systems that react to the changes we create. Gardening initiates changes that affect the soil and therefore our plants.

Nearly every rose book ever written says that roses must have a clay soil to grow to perfection. This emphasis on clay soils is a bit misleading. Clay is consistently recommended mostly because of its ability to hold more water, thus making it less likely that the rose will dry out. Dry rose bushes do not flower or grow well. Another reason clay soils are recommended is because most roses are propagated by budding the desired variety onto a rootstock. Usually the rootstock is either *Rosa multiflora* or *Rosa canina*, species that grow best in heavier soils. However, many of the roses that the northern gardener plants, such as the *rugosa* rose and Scotch rose, actually prefer lighter soils when on their own roots. The important point to remember is that roses must have a consistent supply of water and nutrients to grow to their potential. Virtually any type of soil can successfully grow roses if it is well drained and has enough organic content for good water retention and nutrient supply.

There are very few soils that require no work on the gardener's part to meet these conditions. Most of us live with soils that are not ideal. They may be low in organic material, they may have a heavy clay texture that does not allow the free passage of air and water, or they may be a very light soil that will not hold water and dries out quickly. Your task as gardener is to improve those conditions. Depending upon your soil, this task can be simple or herculean.

SOIL ACIDITY

One of the most important characteristics of soil is also one of the easiest conditions to alter. The soil of any site has a certain level of acidity or alkalinity, called its pH level. The pH of a substance can range from 0 to 14, with 7 being neutral. Most plants grow in the 4 to 9 range. The ideal pH level for roses is 6 to 7. Within this range the rose can make best use of the elements available in the soil. If the soil drops in pH (becoming more acidic) or rises in pH (becoming more alkaline), certain elements become chemically bonded and therefore unavailable to the plants. You can find out your soil's pH by having it tested. If it is too acidic, add lime or gypsum to correct the problem. If it is too alkaline, add sulfur or iron sulfate to lower the pH. Your soil test should tell you the correct amount of these additives to bring your pH to the desired level. Most departments of agriculture will perform soil tests, or you can do these tests yourself using reasonably priced kits. Getting a soil test done is simple, yet it continually surprises me how few people take the time to do it. Without an accurate soil test you are only guessing your soil's acidity level and playing roulette with your garden's health.

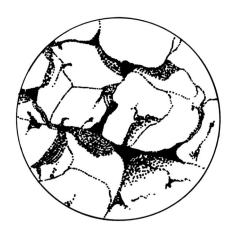

Enlarged view of sand particles

SOIL TEXTURE

"Digging your hands into the earth" is a well-used phrase that deserves closer scrutiny. This phrase evokes images of seeds dropped into hoed trenches, roots settled into their new homes – in essence, the nurturing so central to good gardening. Yet this phrase concerns the texture of soil, and indeed, a soil's texture is of prime importance for good growth.

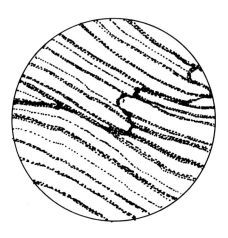

Enlarged view of clay particles

Soils are divided into two general classifications: clay soils and sandy soils. Clay soils contain a high percentage of minerals such as mica and feldspar. These minerals are made of tiny, flat plates that adhere closely together, making it difficult for water and air to penetrate between them. To break up a clay, it is necessary to mix in large amounts of coarse-textured organic material. These odd-shaped chunks hold the clay particles apart, creating spaces in which water and air can circulate. Because most roots grow near the surface of the soil, it is best to work most of your organic material into this layer. Here the roots will benefit from the increased oxygen supplies and the nutrients that the break-down of the organic matter creates.

Sandy soils have the opposite problem. Sand soils are composed of grains of silica, or quartz. These are irregular and have spaces between them that air and water can pass through freely. If there is little organic matter in a sand soil, it dries out quickly.

Water passing slowly through a clay soil dissolves the surfaces of the mineral particles, releasing elements in the process. The particles of a sandy soil, however, do not dissolve easily in water because of their composition. As well, the rapid passage of water through sandy soil tends to quickly drain away what few available nutrients there are. For these reasons, sandy soils tend to be less fertile. However, the addi-

The coarse nature of sand particles allows the free passage of air and water. The flat particles of a clay soil pack tightly together making it difficult for air and water to penetrate.

tion of organic material can rapidly solve this problem. Indeed, some of the best soils in the world are soils composed of sand and fine organic particles. The combination of good drainage and the nutrient- and water-holding capacities of the organic matter create excellent conditions for good growth. As well, loose soils composed of sands and gravels are easier to work with than clay soils.

Most garden soils lie somewhere between the extremes of pure clay and pure sand. In any case, the solution for improving your soil lies in the addition of organic material. Why is organic material so important? Why not simply add the nutrients we need with chemical fertilizers?

Organic material comes from the bodies of plants and animals. When broken down by the soil's microorganisms the elements contained in them are released and combine with water percolating through the soil. This nutrient-laden "soup" feeds your roses. If you examine the roots of a plant, note how the fine roots work their way through the pieces of organic material. They know where the "soup" is being served.

Two well-known sources of organic matter are manure and compost. Another valuable soil conditioner available to most gardeners is peat moss. Its fine fibers have been chemically pickled by centuries of immersion in very acidic water. Although it contains few nutrients, it breaks down slowly and helps hold both water and air effectively in soil for many years. Shredded bark and other forest-industry byproducts are also valuable. Sources such as leaves, grass clippings and prunings are thrown out by countless people, cities and businesses every day. Wise gardeners let it be known that they will accept any clean organic "waste." Properly composted, these wastes will add texture to your soil and will make digging your hands into the earth that much easier.

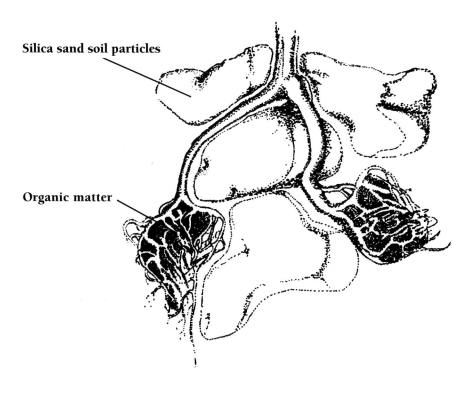

Silica sand soil particles

Organic matter

Fine root hairs surround and penetrate organic matter in the soil, where water is abundant and where the complex process of decay releases nutrients.

MULCHES

I do not garden without mulches. A clean cultivated garden is an unnatural and often hostile environment for a plant. In hot, dry weather it becomes a desert; the surface absorbs and gives off immense quantities of heat and loses moisture rapidly. Rains can cause erosion, and the surface layer can become packed from the impact of raindrops. After a rain, the sun can bake the muddy soil into a hard shell, reducing oxygen levels in the root zone and leading to even worse erosion problems in the next rainfall.

Most plants prefer a "forest floor" type of environment. In a healthy forest, the mulch layer is an equalizer. A mulch on your garden acts in the same way. Its insulating qualities temper the heat of summer and the cold of winter. Mulch absorbs and disperses the impact of falling raindrops, eliminating erosion and preventing soil bacteria and fungi from splashing up onto plants where they can sometimes cause problems. The continual activity by worms, insects and other life encouraged by mulch also creates a network of pathways, which increases the availability of oxygen to the roots. Perhaps most important, an organic mulch provides a flourishing environment for the numerous insects and microscopic plants and animals that are necessary to a healthy soil. Organic matter is continually broken down in such an active community. This breakdown of organic matter releases nutrients into the soil where it can be used by plant roots.

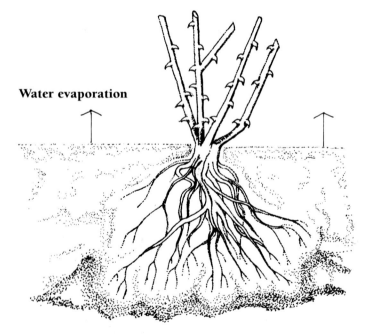

Water evaporation

A clean cultivated soil loses water rapidly in warm weather and roots must penetrate deeply to obtain water.

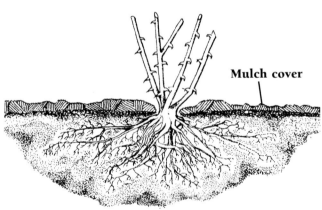

Mulch cover

A mulch cover on the soil reduces evaporation and helps create a wicking effect that keeps water levels evenly distributed throughout the soil. This allows the development of more fine feeding roots near the surface, where soil activity is highest and nutrients most concentrated.

Whenever you add a large amount of organic material to the soil, it is important to realize that the breakdown of that mulch will require nitrogen. Nitrogen fertilizers will provide this, although at the expense of some of the soil's microscopic life. However, if a good quantity of well-made compost is incorporated on the surface just before adding your mulch, it will provide enough nitrogen and will further improve your soil's texture and fertility. If the mulch layer is not worked into the soil, the nitrogen requirements will be smaller. Once this mulch "stabilizes," simply add new mulch on the surface every year or two and the system will not overtax nitrogen supplies. This gradual layering mimics the annual addition of leaves to the forest floor.

Inorganic mulches such as solid plastic sheeting exclude oxygen from the soil and should not be used. Modern landscape fabrics allow passage of water and air and will keep weed growth down, but I have two major objections to them. They are a nightmare if you want to work your soil, and pulling them up after a few years in the ground can be a job to tax the patience of any gardener. Worst of all, they are created from nonrenewable oil products. It is bad enough that we squander these precious resources on things we consider essential, but to cover our gardens with them is not only unnecessary but unforgivable.

PROVIDING NUTRIENTS

A healthy soil seethes with life. The soil's plants and animals go through countless cycles of birth and death. This cycle's waste products, when dissolved in the soil's water, are the nutrients your rose uses for growth. Bacteria and worm and insect manures are the prime sources of a soil's ability to nourish plants.

To create active soils, you often have to "kick-start" your soil with organic materials and sources of nitrogen. The organic material can be thought of as a storehouse filled with the elements that were used to construct the plants that make it up. The nitrogen is the key that starts the process of unlocking that storehouse, for it is at the microscopic level that the breakdown begins. If adequate levels of nitrogen are available, one-celled creatures such as bacteria begin to digest the fibers and other tissues in the organic matter. Soon multicelled creatures consume bacteria. Small insects consume these creatures, and so on. As long as there is a steady addition of organic material, the process will continue. If no more organic matter is added, the nitrogen levels will increase until the existing organic material is consumed; the levels then will fall off quickly. If large amounts of organic matter are added, the process will slow because there will be a temporary shortage of nitrogen for the bacteria. By maintaining a steady input of organic matter and nitrogen-rich materials, you can keep your soil humming with activity, a soil that can provide the nutrients your roses need to grow and flower well.

If you treat your soil as if it is simply a medium into which you introduce needed elements in the form of soluble fertilizers, you will gradually degrade your soil. Without sufficient organic material, the water-soluble elements in the fertilizers pass quickly through the soil. Your plant will absorb a certain amount of them, but most will leach out through the soil, ending up in the water table and eventually in the rivers. This excessive use of fertilizers has caused severe problems in lakes and rivers in many agricultural areas.

Although your plant will have absorbed some of the nitrogen, phosphorus and potassium from the chemical fertilizer, these fertilizers do not contain the numerous micronutrients that are also essential to proper plant growth. Micronutrients are those elements that are needed only in small quantities. They are, however, absolutely necessary. Without the tiny portions of zinc, sulfur, selenium, boron and other such elements, the complex molecules that make up the plant's tissues cannot be constructed. It's like having the steel to build a bridge without the bolts to hold the pieces together. It is the organic material in your soil that contributes most of these micronutrients.

Another consideration when using chemical fertilizers is their acidifying nature. As most fertilizers dissolve, they acidify the soil. For naturally acidic soils, it is essential that the pH be adjusted to compensate for this process. Many gardeners complain to me of not getting adequate growth even though they are fertilizing heavily. When I ask whether they have added lime recently, their usual reaction is "I didn't know it was necessary." By adding lime to their soil, they could use a fraction of the fertilizer and have much better growth.

Nitrogen is very important in the formation of the proteins necessary to build stems, leaves and roots. Other elements are important too, but nitrogen is more difficult to keep in the soil. It disperses into the air and is quickly leached away by rains. This instability creates a constant need to replenish nitrogen in the soil and makes it the focus of most fertilizer programs.

If you are committed to raising healthy, vigorous roses, you must be committed to building soil, for the former is dependent upon the latter. Though the soil's activities are complex, the practical solutions to fertilizing your rose beds are simple. Innumerable materials can be used to build better soils, but essentially we are talking about manures and composts.

THE MAGIC OF MANURE

Most people would hardly consider manure a worthwhile topic of conversation. It is safe to say, however, that without using manure as a fertilizer, humans would still be hunter-gatherers. The conversion of human culture to an agricultural base required soils whose fertility could be sustained. The discovery of using manure as fertilizer to increase crop yields and maintain soil texture made the agricultural revolution sustainable.

As food passes through an animal, its composition is altered. Fresh manure contains a high percentage of ammonia. This is partly why manure has such a pungent smell. Ammonia is high in nitrogen and is a readily available source for plants. As soon as the manure is exposed to the air, however, the ammonia begins to evaporate and the nitrogen is lost to the atmosphere. As well, rain percolates through the manure, leaching out the nitrogen. So while fresh manure is a good source of nitrogen, older, exposed manure, although still valuable for its organic content, is not nearly as valuable as fertilizer. A good farmer will work fresh manure quickly into the soil so that the nitrogen will not be lost.

You should be cautious of fresh manure, however. The ammonia it gives off poses a danger to plants. Plants are nitrogen hogs, and will absorb nitrogen as long as it is available. Fresh manure near a plant's roots provides a tremendous quantity of nitrogen. As long as adequate water is available to the plant it will be able to handle the nitrogen. However, if water is limited in any way, the nitrogen will form salts in the plant's tissues, which will burn the plant up. Manure also contains the bane of gardeners everywhere – weeds. Many weed seeds pass through animals without harm. Once put into the soil with the manure, they have not only a place to grow but the nutrition to grow well.

Because many gardeners today live in urban environments, the close connections between farmyard manure and the garden have essentially disappeared. Many gardeners may have only bagged manure available to them. Although often variable in quality and usually pricey, bagged manure is still a valuable soil enricher. It is also usually heat-treated to destroy weed seeds. The bagged manure may lack the nutrient value of a fresh pie from an alfalfa-fed Holstein cow, but it will still work magic.

No matter our source, if we want to use manure to best advantage we need to convert the nitrogen to a more stable form and to eliminate the problem of weed seeds. The answer is to make compost.

THE MIRACLE OF COMPOST

If you know how to make a complete, balanced compost, you do not need any other plant food. Well-made compost should contain all the nutrients needed for healthy growth. It will contain the bacteria, fungi and other microscopic life that work to control diseases in soil, and it will provide valuable organic matter.

The secret of good compost lies in balance. Bacteria in a compost pile feed on the carbon in the organic material and convert it into energy. The bacteria require nitrogen, phosphorus and potassium, among other elements, to accomplish this task. Although phosphorus and potassium are available in the organic material, nitrogen is usually in low supply. We need to add nitrogen to the pile. Fresh manure is the most common source of nitrogen for compost makers, but it is not always available. Many nitrogen-rich materials can be purchased at local animal feed-stores. These include linseed meal, soyameal, cottonseed meal, blood meal, bonemeal and feather meal. If you live near the sea you may be able to obtain fish or shellfish waste. Any of these, or similar high-protein materials, provide the nitrogen necessary to get your compost working.

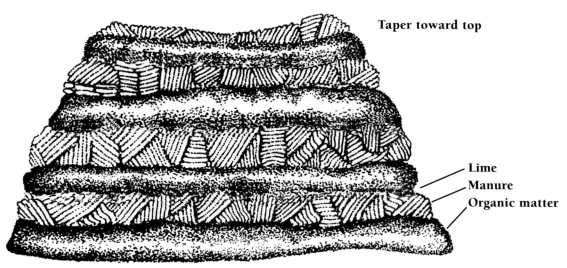

Taper toward top

Lime
Manure
Organic matter

Cross-section of compost heap

A balance must be struck between the carbon and the nitrogen in the pile. The proper ratio for optimum compost activity is 30 carbon to 1 nitrogen. To achieve a healthy compost pile with a well-balanced carbon/nitrogen ratio, start as follows.

Spread your organic material into a layer approximately 1 ft. (30 cm) thick. This might include materials like old hay, vegetable peelings, leaves (preferably shredded) or weeds. On top of this, spread a layer of fresh manure approximately 3 in. (8 cm) thick. If you cannot obtain manure, put a thinner layer of whatever organic nitrogen source you can obtain. If you are unable to obtain any organic sources of nitrogen, sprinkle a fertilizer such as urea (42-0-0) very lightly over your organic matter. Sprinkle a few shovelfuls of earth over the whole lot. This earth contains enough soil bacteria to act as a starter for the breakdown process, although many argue that it is not necessary. If you want a sweet (high pH) compost, add a shovelful of lime. Repeat this layering until the pile is about 4 ft. (1.2 m) tall. As you layer your pile, be sure to add enough water to make it thoroughly moist but not soggy.

Once your pile is built, turn it regularly. Turning a compost heap puts oxygen into the pile. This oxygen is vital to keep the bacteria active. Some compost heaps never break down properly due to lack of oxygen. Turning every day or two is ideal, but few of us have that kind of time. If you can turn your pile once a week, or at most once every two weeks, the compost will work well. After one or two turnings, your compost heap should be steaming hot inside. A properly balanced and aerated compost pile will reach temperatures of 160°F (72°C). These high temperatures destroy the weed seeds and any harmful diseases that may be present in the materials. Remember that the size of your pile is not very important. Even a small compost pile will work well if there is a proper carbon/nitrogen balance and if it is damp and turned regularly. If space is limited or tidiness a concern, there are many compost makers available that are easy to use.

Build your compost heap like a giant sandwich, layering nitrogen-rich materials between the bulk of organic materials. Keep the pile moist and turn often to introduce oxygen into the pile. The layer of lime should be a light sprinkling, with no depth. Too much lime will raise the pH to undesirable levels.

Once it cools, your compost is ready to use. In the garden it will continue to break down, and as it does so, it will slowly release the nitrogen and other elements your plants need. If your quantities are limited, use it as a side dressing around your plants or incorporate some in your planting holes. If you have larger quantities, use it as a general top dressing on your garden. If you make composting a regular part of your garden program you will see the results in healthy growth and good flowering.

WEEDING

Ask a gardener what they like least about gardening and inevitably the answer is weeding. It is the subject books on gardening tend to avoid. After all, who wants to talk about work when you can talk about the scintillating colors, the exotic fragrances, the joys and beauties that gardening can create? But the truth is, a garden's beauty cannot unfold without weeding. Planting, watering, pruning, feeding and weeding are tasks that must be done so that we can enjoy the results.

I enjoy weeding. After a hectic day I can think of no more relaxing activity than to go into my garden and weed. It allows me to be close to the plants, to touch them, to examine them for any problems, to enjoy them. Gardening for me, as it is for so many, is a spiritual exercise, and far from being repelled by weeding, I find it lends structure and discipline to the experience. At the same time, no one enjoys hacking at overgrown weeds, or working in gardens that resemble abandoned hay fields. The longer the weeding is neglected, the more work it will need to bring the garden back under control. The secret to keeping weeds at a manageable stage is working with properly prepared ground and keeping to a regular schedule of maintenance.

Attitudes toward weeds vary from the relaxed to the compulsive. Whatever your attitude, keep in mind that weeds can teach us valuable lessons about our soil and our management techniques. Weeds are simply plants that are growing where we don't want them, but they are not a homogeneous group. Weeds differ in their habits and needs. By examining which weeds are growing in your garden, you can often discover whether your soil is too acidic or too alkaline, if cultivation is required, if the ground is lacking in certain nutrients and a host of other information. Turn weeding from a nuisance into an opportunity to learn more about your garden.

SOIL PREPARATION

Weeding begins before you plant your first rose. If you are starting with a new piece of ground, the first order of business is to remove as many perennial weeds as possible, being sure to remove the roots to prevent the weed from regrowing. Although it is not exciting work, every hour you spend preparing your site will be repaid many times over in the future. Once the initial preparation is complete, you may want to add compost or manure. (Keep in mind that manure will contain weed seeds.) Once you have planted your roses, seriously consider mulching with a layer of organic material such as shredded bark or other materials that do not contain weed seeds. Many seeds need light to germinate, and the mulch will prevent light from reaching them. A thick layer of mulch will also keep many seeds from reaching the surface if they do germinate. Some will always manage to make it to sunlight, and any perennial roots that remain will send up shoots, but these are easily pulled in a mulched garden, an advantage that will be appreciated by those who have had to cultivate hard, baked ground, in which the weed roots are nearly impossible to remove. A mulch keeps the ground looser and better aerated, making it easy to remove both the top and the root of the weed.

When planning your garden, remember that an isolated plant in a lawn is difficult to maintain. Grass moves in quickly, and keeping your plant free of weeds can be a chore. If you can plant in groupings or beds, you will be able to keep the ground between the plants more easily cultivated. This makes lawn mowing much easier as well. Rather than having to push under a bush from all sides, the mower can simply follow the edge of the bed. This edge should be cut with a spade each spring to prevent grass or other weed roots from moving into the bed. Leave a cut face at the edge; this will tend to "air prune" any roots moving toward the bed. If your garden plan calls for individual plants on the lawn, keep the edge of the cultivated area away from the plants. This will allow you to easily maintain that edge.

WEED MANAGEMENT

Weed new gardens often, particularly during the first few months. At this stage the weeds are not well established and are easy to deal with. If you wait, the roots will quickly spread, and pulling or hoeing becomes increasingly difficult. Begin weeding early as well in established gardens. The spring and early summer are periods of intense growth. By getting to the weeding early you will not have as big a job, and you will be able to relax during the summer when your roses are magnificent and you are warm and lazy.

Most weeding can be done in a mulched garden by simply pulling weeds out by hand. This requires only your hands and gloves, and perhaps the help of a three-pronged hand cultivator. If you prefer to keep your garden clean cultivated, there are several tools to aid you in your work. If you must choose only one tool to have, make it a hoe. This age-old simple device has never been replaced as the number-one gardening aid. Several designs are on the market today, including hoes with triangular blades, push-pull types or ones with open U-shaped blades. The common hoe with a more or less rectangular blade is still the most popular design and, I would argue, the most useful.

Good hoeing is an acquired art. Most people hold a hoe nearly horizontally and hack at the ground. This destroys both the hoe and your arms. A hoe should be held nearly vertically so that the blade cuts away thin slices of ground. Cut these slices from the uncultivated ground, pulling the loosened earth toward you as you work. Walk forward, working in a regular pattern of strokes from right to left or vice versa. If you work as you walk backward, with the blade pushing into the harder earth, you will be working twice as hard with poorer results. Such instructions may sound fussy, but you will be surprised at how much easier and productive hoeing is when done properly.

Weeds can be managed with the aid of chemicals. Called herbicides, these chemicals prevent weed seeds from germinating or destroy existing weeds. The newest generation of herbicides works by interfering with the normal transfer of materials in the plant, killing the plant down to the root tips. Essentially these materials are labor replacers. Labor in agriculture is expensive, and using herbicides lowers expenses.

There is, however, a hidden cost in herbicides. Many of these materials work their way through the soil and into the groundwater, where they then show up in wells, in rivers, and ultimately in the oceans. Areas treated with herbicides often cannot be planted with certain crops for years after the chemicals have been applied. Careless use of herbicides results in the loss of neighboring plants and contamination of soil and water. Children who play on lawns treated with herbicides can develop allergic reactions or illness. It is difficult to measure these hidden costs, but we need to carefully consider the consequences of using herbicides.

Herbicides are another unknown quantity in the chemical onslaught we are inflicting on the Earth. Modern insecticides were introduced after World War II, and their use has accelerated at an alarming rate since then. The harvest of that headlong rush into chemical management is now being reaped. Our water, air and soil are polluted. Plants, animals and humans are being affected in serious ways. Even our food is contaminated.

If we want to clean up our environment, we must make decisions that reflect that commitment. Herbicides are *not* needed in a garden, and I feel they have no place in gardening or agriculture. Any possible benefit we gain by their use is far outweighed by the consequences to ourselves, our children and all life on Earth.

PLANTING

When you purchase a rose bush, you hold in your hand the potential for many years of satisfaction and pleasure. To insure that this potential is secure, you need to properly plant your rose.

The first order of business is to be sure that your rose does not dry out while you prepare the planting hole. As soon as you get your rose, plunge the rootball in water for several hours. This will allow the plant to absorb as much water as it can hold. After the roots have sat in the water for up to 12 hours, take the bush out for planting. If you cannot

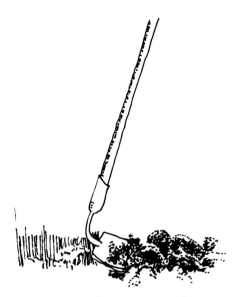

Hoe in a regular sequence of strips, always pulling undisturbed soil toward you as you proceed forward. Keep your hoe nearly vertical so that you slice rather than chop the soil.

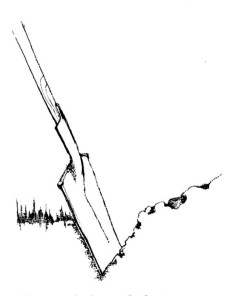

Edge your beds regularly. A steep vertical edge will tend to discourage, at least temporarily, grass and weeds from growing into the bed.

plant it immediately, bury the roots in a trench in your garden or in damp bark or sawdust until you are ready. Remember that even a few minutes in a dry spot, especially in the sun, can mean disaster.

Very often the rose you purchase will be a container-grown plant. If this is the case, be sure that any long, spiraling roots are teased out when you plant such a rose. If the roots have become a dense mass on the outside of the rootball and separating them is difficult, make several shallow cuts with a knife up and down the rootball. This will force the formation of smaller roots, which will grow into the new soil. Rootbound plants, if not unbound, will often not grow into the surrounding soil, and in the worst of cases can strangle themselves to death. Rootbound plants are also easily pushed out of the ground by frostheave in northern areas.

When you prepare the planting hole, first remove any weeds, particularly their roots, from in and around the site. Dig a hole that is wide enough for the entire root system to be spread out, and dig it deep enough so that the roots will be entirely underground. Most roses are budded roses. Such roses have a bud of the variety inserted under the bark of a rootstock. At the union of the rootstock and variety a bulbous crook is formed. This union should be buried at least 4 in. (10 cm) below the soil surface. The soil will protect the union from the more severe winter temperatures and will help prevent suckering from the rootstock. Roses grown from cuttings or layers can be planted at the same depth as they were previously growing, or slightly deeper if you wish.

If you have a reasonably loose loam, it is an advantage to work compost or well-rotted manure into the hole. A handful of bonemeal is also advisable, as this gives the plant a long-term source of phosphorus, which is needed for root development. If you wish to use peat moss, be sure that it is well moistened before you put it in the hole. Be careful not to have the peat moss account for more than one-quarter of the volume of the soil, as this may be too light a mix and may cause the hole to dry out quickly. This is especially important with heavier clay soils. These denser soils will tend to draw water away from the lighter soil within the hole. Your rose will not receive adequate water. If you have a clay soil, it is usually better to replace around your rose roots the same clay you dug out of the hole. Adding some compost and bonemeal is fine. After the rose is planted, place the greater part of your compost and organic materials at the surface, where the feeder roots will form and make best use of these nutrients.

When planting the rose, be sure to work the soil around the root system so that no air pockets remain. These delay the formation of the smaller roots, which are so important in establishing your rose. Once you have worked the soil to the top, tamp firmly with your hands or feet. Leave a slight depression on the surface and fill this with water. Once it soaks in, fill the depression again until you are sure that the entire hole is completely saturated. If you are mulching, spread the mulch on the surface and give one more watering.

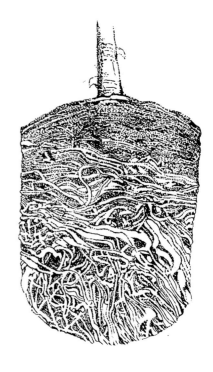

Potted roses can form masses of spiraling roots on the outside of the rootball. These roots must be teased or cut to ensure that the new roots will grow into the surrounding soil.

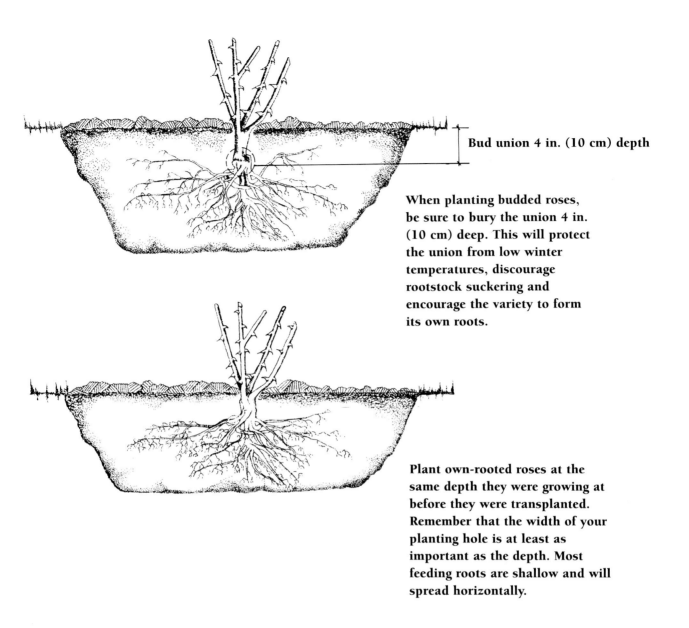

Bud union 4 in. (10 cm) depth

When planting budded roses, be sure to bury the union 4 in. (10 cm) deep. This will protect the union from low winter temperatures, discourage rootstock suckering and encourage the variety to form its own roots.

Plant own-rooted roses at the same depth they were growing at before they were transplanted. Remember that the width of your planting hole is at least as important as the depth. Most feeding roots are shallow and will spread horizontally.

The most important part of establishing a new rose is watering. Keep a regular schedule of watering, giving the rose the equivalent of at least 1 or 1 1/2 in. (2 or 4 cm) of rain a week. That is a fair amount of water. Be sure to soak the hole well. A few sprays on the surface will not do your rose any good. It takes more water than most people think to thoroughly soak down to the bottom of a planting hole. If you are faithful about watering, your rose will repay you with good growth and more prolific blooming. Even a weak plant will thrive if given enough water. However, a plant can be overwatered, particularly in heavier clay soils. If the roots are kept too wet, they will lack sufficient oxygen. Common sense is your best guide in such situations.

After planting your rose you may wish to prune it back. Be sure to read the section "Pruning the New Rose" for instructions.

PRUNING

Pruning begins before you even buy your roses. It begins in your living room when you are curled up in your easychair deciding what rose to put in which space. The roses you choose all have distinctive growth patterns. If you have a space where you want a low-growing variety, don't put in a vigorous variety with the idea that you can keep it pruned down. Plant a rose that will best suit the space. If you don't, you will constantly be fighting against the natural growth pattern of the plant. You will create far more work than is necessary, and the results will never be as satisfying. Keep in mind that pruning is always a dwarfing process. To better understand what happens when you prune, it helps to visualize how a plant works.

Inside your rose, water and nutrients are absorbed by the roots and flow up the stems to the top of the plant. The top then uses the water and nutrients to make food, which is sent throughout the upper portion of the plant. Any leftovers are sent down to feed the root system. Pruning removes potential leaf surface from your plant. The leaves are the food-production centers of the plant, turning sunlight, water and nutrients into what we call sap. Stems, to an extent, are also involved in the production of food. When you remove parts of the plant with your pruning shears, you are reducing a portion of this "food factory" and thereby limiting the plant's capacity for growth.

Pruning keeps a rose in prime condition by allowing it to form new stems and leaves.

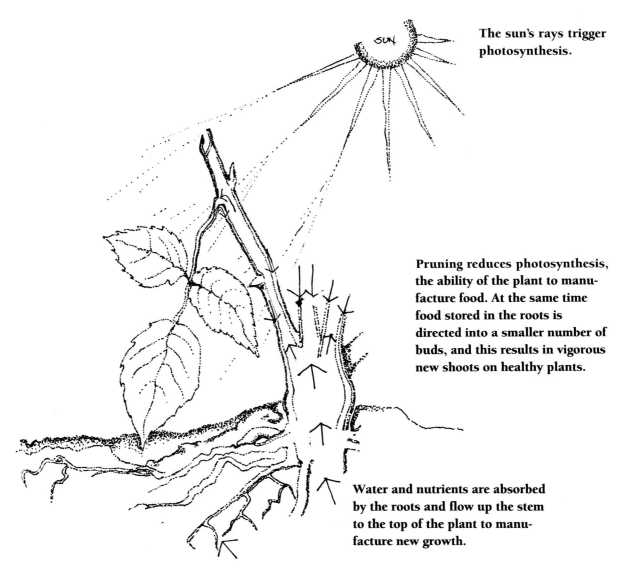

The sun's rays trigger photosynthesis.

Pruning reduces photosynthesis, the ability of the plant to manufacture food. At the same time food stored in the roots is directed into a smaller number of buds, and this results in vigorous new shoots on healthy plants.

Water and nutrients are absorbed by the roots and flow up the stem to the top of the plant to manufacture new growth.

Pruning redirects growth in the plant. When portions of a plant are removed, it uses its remaining buds to form new stems and leaves. The food necessary to grow new parts comes, for the most part, from the root system, where much of the plants' food reserves are stored. If the root system is well established and has a good supply of food, the plant will be able to quickly replace what it has lost and even grow beyond that point. If a plant is weak and is severely pruned, it will take much more time to regain the capacity for growth it had before it was pruned. If the top growth cannot occur quickly enough to replace the food supply in the root system, the roots will starve and eventually the plant will die. It is essential, therefore, that pruning be kept to the minimum necessary to accomplish your purpose. Any more may needlessly weaken your plant.

However, don't be frightened into inaction, worried that you might harm your roses by pruning. Pruning is a useful art, allowing you to keep your roses in prime condition. By and large, the rose is a very forgiving and resilient plant.

Before

After

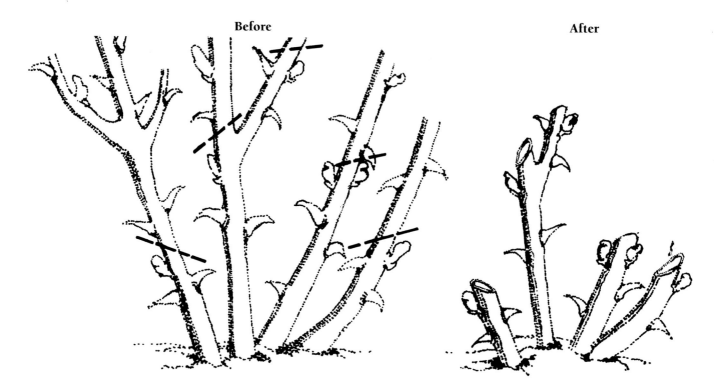

TOOLS OF THE TRADE

To do a good job of pruning, you have to have the right tools. This does not involve a major investment. Although the occasional fifty-year-old *rugosa* rose may warrant a chainsaw, the only tools generally needed are the common hand-held pruning shears or secateurs and, for large old canes, a pair of long-handled lopping shears.

Pruning shears come in several designs and in a wide range of prices. If you are a serious gardener, spend a little extra. A precision-crafted pair of pruning shears that is kept sharp is a joy to use. A poorly made pair will cause nothing but aggravation, will not cut cleanly or easily and will probably have to be replaced much sooner than a well-built pair. The best types even come with replaceable parts. (Quality, of course, should govern your choice of all gardening equipment.)

Another tool you may find useful is a small hand-held pruning saw. With their thin, sharp blades, these are excellent for getting into hard-to-prune areas or for removing branches that are too large for shears. Most of these saws cut on the pull stroke. For delicate work on smaller wood, a thin-bladed sharp knife is often the ideal tool. It is light, easy to maneuver and capable of smooth, clean cuts.

Last but definitely not least are gloves. Going into a rose bush without gloves borders on masochism. You can bet you're going to come out with blood on your hands, or worse, needle-thin thorns imbedded in your skin; if these are not immediately removed, they will remind you of your foolishness for many days. The rose represents both the joy and the pain of love in literature. To a rose grower this analogy needs no explanation.

Pruning back a newly planted rose results in several stocky and vigorous shoots. Pruning to outside buds helps keep the center of the bush open.

PRUNING THE NEW ROSE

A well-grown and well-handled young rose has a healthy root system endowed with numerous small, fine roots and several sturdy stems filled with the food necessary for next season's growth. Such a young rose, if planted in good soil and kept watered, should grow well and require only moderate pruning when planted. Unfortunately, many of the roses that you purchase have been underfed, grown under poor conditions, dug carelessly with a machine set at an improper digging depth or simply allowed to dry out somewhere along the often tortuous route from the nursery to your garden.

The excitement you feel when your new roses arrive often fades when you open the package to find plants with a few dry roots and perhaps some mold growing where the tops were pruned. This scenario should be followed by emergency action. Soak your plants for at least 12 hours but not more than 24 hours. Cut off all dead wood and the top stems to only a few buds. Because the roots are going to be very slow to absorb water, they will not be able to adequately supply it to all the emerging buds and the top will most likely wither, often followed by the death of the entire plant. By concentrating all its energies into a small area close to the root system, the plant can usually supply enough water and food to the remainder for vigorous growth.

With luck your new roses will not be in such a sorry condition. For the average new rose a less rigorous pruning may do. However, as a general rule it is best to prune back a new planted rose fairly severely. By doing so you concentrate the growth in the remaining buds, which will tend to produce several strong shoots rather than many spindly ones.

When pruning your new rose, make your cuts so that the last bud will grow outward. If you leave an inward-facing bud, you will often end up with crossed branches that will need to be pruned again later. Make your cuts so that they slope slightly away from the bud. Cut fairly close to the bud so that you will not end up with a dead stub, which can become infected with canker, but not so close that the bud will be in danger of drying out. An eighth of an inch (3 or 4 mm) is about the right length.

Examine the roots before planting and prune off any dead ones. If the ends of any roots are ragged or torn, prune them off cleanly. Do not prune any more than necessary from the root system. The more roots available to the plant, the more water and nutrients it will be able to absorb and the quicker it will be able to recover from transplanting.

MAINTENANCE PRUNING

Once your new rose has established itself, a program of maintenance can begin. The question of when to prune has always been a source of debate. Successful pruning can be accomplished in either late fall or early spring. If pruning in late fall, wait until the leaves turn color and start to fall. The longer you wait, the more food will be delivered to the root system and the more vigorous your rose will be in the spring.

Pruning too early in the fall can initiate soft late growth that may not withstand hard frost and will winterkill. Most growers still prefer early spring for their pruning, and I think a good case can be made for delaying pruning till spring in the northern garden. Many of the roses we grow in the north will kill back a certain percentage each winter. If you wait till spring to prune, it will be easier to assess the amount of damage that the plant has suffered, and the plant can be pruned accordingly. The dead portions can be removed and the remainder shaped. However, spring can often be a very busy time for gardeners. If you know that time will be at a premium in the spring, by all means prune in the fall. The hardier varieties will probably not suffer. Just leave the more tender types till spring.

When you begin pruning, first take out dead or diseased portions and remove any crossed branches. If your rose has already grown larger than you wish, remove the weaker thin wood and cut back the top to the desired height. When thinning out wood, cut back to the next branch. This will create a more natural appearance and will avoid numerous stubs, which give the plant a butchered look and invite disease. The top branches should be cut so that an equal space is given to each branch. Cut to a bud that will grow into the empty spaces. As the shrub types age, it is advisable to cut out the oldest canes. This will continually rejuvenate the bush, leaving younger, more floriferous wood and helping to keep the plant within reasonable limits.

Many people feel incompetent when it comes to pruning. It is perhaps the most mysterious and least understood of horticultural endeavors. Indeed, the sorry results of unsympathetic pruning can be viewed on any street. Conversely, the result of neglecting pruning can be an overgrown tangle. If you are unsure of how to begin, try stepping back from your subject. Think how your plant should look. Is your rose a vigorous, rounded shrub? Is it a tall, wiry climber? Visualize the perfect plant (of the kind you are dealing with) and superimpose it on your specimen. Pick out and retain the main structural elements. Eliminate the growth that is superfluous to the shape you desire or that extends beyond the limits you want to impose on it. If you can work with the natural growth pattern of your subject, you will be able to achieve a harmonious result. If you are constantly fighting against the plant's growth pattern, the results will look stilted. As with so many things in life, experience is the best teacher. The more pruning you do, the more confident you will become.

PRUNING HEDGES

The first few years are critical when developing hedges. Once you have decided upon the general shape of your hedge, remove the growth that is beyond the imaginary planes of the hedge's sides and top. As the plants continue to grow, your spring pruning will be removing more material each year. It may also be desirable to prune after the first flush of flowering to remove wayward branches. Always be sure to keep the

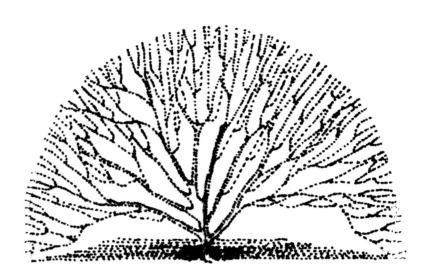

Keep your hedge widest at the base so that the entire leaf surface receives adequate light.

base of the hedge wider than the top so that adequate light is available to the entire surface of the hedge. If you try to maintain a vertically sided hedge, or try to curve the lower edge to form a ball shape, the bottom section will not receive enough light and will become open with only the branches showing.

As the hedge ages, you should systematically remove the oldest canes in the plants. A few canes removed each year will not create large and noticeable holes, and will encourage new and more productive wood to form. Your hedge will flower better, and you will be creating enough space for light and air to reach the inner parts of the hedge.

Roses lend themselves to an informal style of hedge. Although it is possible to create a more formal geometric style with careful attention to pruning, the continual shearing needed to maintain the sharp edges of such a hedge tends to form a rather dense outer "skin," which does not allow good light and air penetration into the interior of the hedge. By pruning too often you will destroy many of the developing flower buds and your hedge will not be as colorful. If you desire a formal hedge, it is probably advisable to stick with plants that lend themselves better to this use.

If you have a sunny area where an informal hedge would be effective, roses can be a choice hedging material. With gentle shaping and careful renewal, you can maintain a cascading wall of color that will be useful and visually exciting.

PRUNING OLDER ROSES

When speaking of hardy roses, we generally mean shrub types. Many of these are vigorous, permanent elements in the landscape and will endure for decades. As they mature they gradually thicken, often becoming very dense. This can result in plants that are really empty shells. The

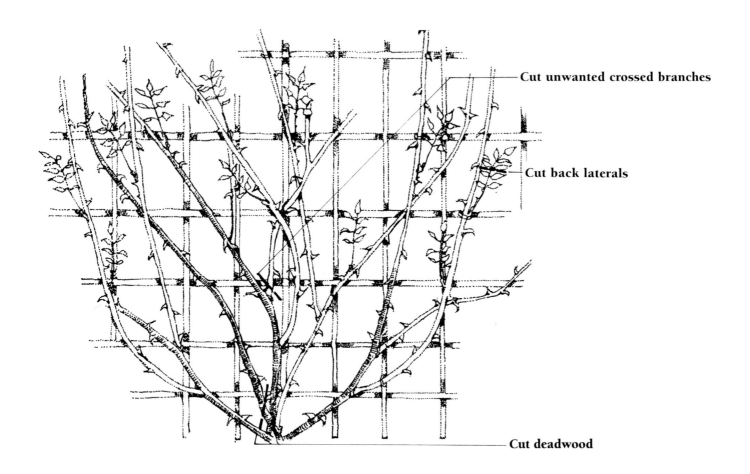

Cut unwanted crossed branches

Cut back laterals

Cut deadwood

center of the bush receives very little light. As a result, no growth occurs on the inside, and only the outside branches put on new growth.

As the pruner, your job is to thin these bushes so that light can penetrate all sections of the plant. Ideally this is an ongoing process, which begins when the plant is young and continues annually. However, you may have to deal with a plant that has been neglected and must be rejuvenated. In the worst of cases it may be advisable to tear out the plant and either replace it or dig out a section of the plant and treat it as a small new plant. If you wish to keep the plant, you should begin by pruning out some of the older canes. This can be a tough job, requiring powerful long-handled shears or a good pruning saw, thick gloves and a great deal of determination. Prune these old canes at ground level. If the plant is very large, prune out some of the canes one year and the remainder the following year. As light penetrates into the plant it will stimulate new growth, which will tend to be more floriferous than the older growth. Gradually cut back the top of the plant as well if you wish to lower the height. Again, this may take a few years. Some old roses can be cut nearly to the ground and will rebound to form a lovely bush, but this treatment can often result in death, particularly for species such as *Rosa foetida* and its hybrids. Patience is definitely called for with such roses.

Keeping older roses vigorous and productive involves removing dead wood, older canes and thin or crossed branches. The top can be cut back to keep the bush tidy and compact. The severity of pruning should be guided by the health of the bush and the desired result.

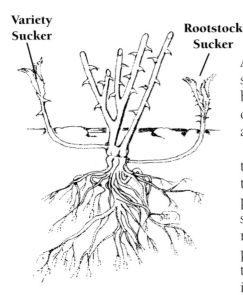

Variety Sucker

Rootstock Sucker

Suckers produced by the rootstock should be removed immediately, for they divert growth from the variety and will not produce the desired flowers. Suckers from the variety can be removed or left, depending on how far you want your rose to spread.

SUCKERING PROBLEMS

A rose can be either on its own roots or budded or grafted onto a rootstock. If your rose is on its own roots, then any suckers that occur from below ground will have the same flowers and growth habits. The vigorous shoots that grow from the base of an own-rooted plant will branch and be the source of many new flowers.

If your rose is budded, however, the suckers that grow from below the bud union will be quite different from the top. It is essential that these suckers be removed as soon as they are noticed. They should be pruned off at the point from which they are growing out of the main stem. If a stub is left, it will usually grow several new shoots from the remaining buds. If pruning with shears is difficult, the shoot can be pressed down at the base until it breaks off the main stem. The injury to the stem can result in infection with crown gall or other diseases, but in actuality it rarely harms the plant and is often the most effective way to deal with suckers. Burying the graft union well below the surface will go a long way toward lessening the incidence of suckering.

FURTHER MAINTENANCE

A few pruning techniques can be used with good effect during the growing season. When a cluster of flowers has finished blooming, that section of the stem does not grow any more. New growth starts from the first vegetative bud below the flower cluster. If the old cluster is pruned off, it will stimulate this bud into active growth and within a few weeks, you can have more bloom. This is effective only on repeating roses. Removing the old blooms will also eliminate the possibility of seeds forming. The plant spends a good deal of energy on seed formation, and when these old blooms are pruned off, the plant has more energy to form new growth. Obviously, if you want rose hips you won't want to practice this technique.

Some roses leave their petals in a messy, brown lump when they have finished blooming. The removal of these spent blooms, or "deadheading" as it is called, will help to maintain a fresh look to the plant and, for the reasons mentioned above, will encourage rapid new growth.

Be on the lookout for problems such as rose galls. These swellings are formed by small insects that lay their eggs in the stems. Upon hatching, the larvae feed on the inside of the stem, causing it to swell. If allowed to complete their life cycle they will infect other roses. Cut out any unnatural swellings as soon as they are noticed. Various infections such as cankers should be cut out as soon as you notice them. These often start on dead wood such as pruning stubs or winter-injured branches. They can quickly work their way into live tissue and cause a great deal of damage if not tended.

4

Insects and Diseases

FROM ABOVE, A CASUAL OBSERVER SEES A GARDEN MURMURING with wind through long-stemmed grasses and fragrant with newly opening roses. But between sand particles, inside last year's decaying stems and on the surfaces of countless leaves and branches, a frenetic drama is taking place with all the cycles of life and death being played out in unbelievably intricate patterns.

It is understandable that many people recoil from insect life. Its forms are so bizarre to us, its patterns so seemingly unrelated to our own. Yet the interested observer who takes the time to gain a better understanding of the insects' life cycles and how they interact in the garden will soon not only develop a fascination for them, but will better appreciate how important the diversity of insect life is to the health of our gardens and ultimately our planet.

There are a number of insects whose lifetime ambition is to suck or chew on rose bushes so that they can obtain all the vitamins, minerals and other necessities needed to produce a new generation to carry on their species. You, the gardener, want to keep your roses healthy so that you can enjoy the sensual splendors they provide. You will need to make some important decisions.

The average manual on roses contains a formidable list of chemical insecticides. Let's take a closer look at what happens to the ecology of a garden when insecticides are used.

Most insecticides kill a wide spectrum of insect species, usually by affecting their nervous or digestive systems. They will kill not only insects inhabiting the leaves and branches of the bush but other

Blackspot appears on leaves in early summer, and can infect an entire shrub.

45

insects and soil microbes as well when the chemicals wash into the soil. These other creatures may be playing important roles in keeping your garden healthy. As rain and sun wash away and degrade the insecticide residues, insect life returns to the sprayed areas. However, with the numbers of many insects reduced, the new balance is quite different.

Every insect has a predator. Without such predators, we would be scraping aphids off our cars in the morning. When we spray our roses we kill not only the pests we want to be rid of but their predators as well. When the surviving pests, or those arriving from other places, start to reinfest the rose bush, few predators remain to keep them under control. This often results in devastatingly high populations of pests, which, if not sprayed again, will do serious damage to your plants. Predators always reproduce more slowly than their food source, otherwise the predators would rapidly eat up their food source and die. In other words, there must always be a population of food (the pests we want to be rid of) present to maintain predator populations. The key to biological control of pests is to be able to maintain high enough populations of predators to keep pests from doing unacceptable damage to your plants.

When you spray insects with an insecticide, most of them will die, but not all. Every creature on Earth is unique, with its own set of characteristics, its own genetic code. So while most insects in a population will be killed by a particular poison, certain individuals may be tolerant to it. If they survive to reproduce, they pass on their tolerance to the new generation. After many generations, entire populations of insects may become tolerant to certain insecticides. This phenomenon is well documented and has caused much concern in conventional agricultural circles. For several years our nursery sprayed its plants with insecticidal soap. This substance is relatively nontoxic to mammals but is effective against many insect species. We noticed after several years that we seemed to need more and more soap to control our aphid populations. It took a while for the truth to sink in. We were creating a race of aphids that could tolerate soap. We had, in effect, outsmarted ourselves. Genetic diversity had triumphed. It was this fact, together with the realization that an annual spray program locked us into a spray-or-die cycle, that convinced us to re-examine our insect control program.

If you wish to adopt a nonchemical approach to gardening, you must first realize that insects are an important part of the garden. Just because it crawls or flies, an insect is not necessarily an unwanted alien. Nearly all insects in your garden are benign or actually help the gardener by keeping other insect populations in check, by pollinating your flowers, by aerating the soil or by performing any number of countless tasks that keep the garden healthy. There will always be some unwanted insects that will feed on our roses. If we are to make a serious commitment to eliminating harmful chemicals from our gardens and our agricultural community, we must change our zero-tolerance approach toward insects. We must accept a certain amount of damage as nature's due. But if you recruit your allies, this damage can be kept inconsequential.

Spiders are among the most useful insect predators.

The health of your plant is of paramount importance in reducing insect problems. A healthy plant reflects a healthy soil and a proper site. If you have looked after the basic requirements of your rose, you will have far fewer problems. An actively growing plant is less subject to insect injury. There is a growing body of evidence that plants under stress are more attractive to insects. This hypothesis is being substantiated by hard data that suggest that plants under stress emit substances and sounds that can be detected by insects. It makes perfect sense that a well-fed plant is more likely to remain healthy. Good parents feed their children well so that they do not suffer from disease. So it should be with our garden charges.

Gardeners constantly seek out varieties with beautiful flowers, unusual color, good vigor or pleasing form. The gardener who is committed to reducing the use of chemicals will pay strict attention to varieties that exhibit good resistance to insects and diseases. Roses differ dramatically in their tolerance to insects. When choosing varieties, select those roses that will make your job easier. It is encouraging that disease and insect resistance are now becoming important criteria for judging new varieties, a trend that is both welcome and long overdue.

As we sit in our gardens enjoying the pleasures they bring, we often revel in the companionship of birds. Whether calling out their melodious songs or enchanting us with their multicolored plumage, they add a charm to a garden that few will fail to appreciate. But birds are much more than colorful ornaments. They are important insect predators and consume nearly their own weight in food every day. This can have a tremendous impact in a garden. By providing good nesting sites and shrubs or trees for perching, you can enlist one of the most effective means of pest control.

Diversity in a garden is a tremendous asset. Most insects go through several phases during their lifetime. By offering an assortment of plants, you can provide sites for predators to complete their life cycles. As an example, in the fall our grapevines harbour clusters of ladybugs, which often number in the hundreds. Ladybugs prey on aphids. Although we do not know why the ladybugs are there (they do not harm the vines), they use the shelter of the grapes to gather and perhaps mate. There are countless similar examples. A healthy garden is a diverse garden.

Lastly, never underestimate your power as a predator. Often an infestation of insects can be easily controlled by simply going into your roses and picking off the culprits. Some small sucking insects can be washed off your roses with a strong spray of water. Once on the ground they are easy prey to the insects that patrol the soil surface. If you know your roses' enemies, you can be a deadly predator.

COMMON INSECT PESTS OF ROSES

If you choose to use biological methods against insects, a better understanding of insect pests is your best weapon. This section contains information on some of the more common pests of roses in northern areas.

By learning about the life cycles of these insects you may discover ways you can interfere with cycles and prevent large populations from building up in your garden. There is no doubt that we can learn from listening to the advice of experts, but remember that anyone with the ability to observe can find new solutions to old problems.

APHIDS

Aphids are perhaps the most common pest of roses. They are small, soft-bodied, usually lime green creatures that puncture the soft new growing tissues with their mouths and suck the leaf juices. Severe infestations will cause the young leaves to curl and dry up. Aphids are nearly always found on the undersides of the leaves near the ends of the shoots. As they feed, they excrete a sticky residue that is attractive to ants. Certain types of ants feed on this "honeydew" and will even protect an aphid colony from other insects. If there is a great deal of "honeydew," it will often appear blackish on the stem's surface as molds and fungi begin to grow on it.

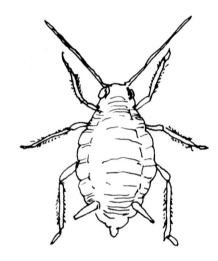

Aphid

Aphids are one of the most prolific insects in existence and also have one of the most amazing life cycles. They overwinter as tiny blackish eggs on the stems, usually near a bud. In the spring small nymphs hatch from the eggs and quickly grow to full size. These first aphids are called stem mothers. They have the fascinating ability to hatch their live young without fertilization from a male. Several generations are produced in this manner. Then a generation is born with wings. These winged aphids, called migrants, fly to other plants, some to the same species of plant, others to a summer host plant, usually an annual of some kind. These continue to produce generations of unfertilized young throughout the summer. As the days grow shorter a generation is produced that contains both winged females and winged males. The females, called fall migrants, fly to the kind of plant on which they started in the spring, then give birth to wingless females, which must be fertilized by the males to produce eggs. The eggs are laid around the buds and crevices of the plant. In the spring these hatch out and the cycle is complete.

Each aphid is theoretically capable of producing millions of aphids by the end of its cycle. The reason we are not swimming in aphids is because so many other insects and birds consume aphids. Early in the spring small solitary spiders can be observed catching and eating aphids. Soon such predators as the small gall midge and the larvae of the syrphid fly begin feeding on them. As spring progresses, the most efficient enemy of the aphid appears. When aphids begin to multiply, adult ladybugs arrive at the aphid colonies and lay their eggs. After about two weeks, tiny, opaque and ravenous larvae hatch and begin feeding. They hold the aphids in their large mandibles and suck their insides out. In only a few days these larvae grow to nearly twenty times their original size and eliminate the colony of aphids. They move from colony to colony until they reach full size. They then form a hardened shell and pupate. In two weeks or so they emerge as the winged ladybugs that most everyone recognizes. They are rounded beetles, usually red or yellow with several dark spots on their wings. Although they eat some aphids at this stage, it is their young that are every aphid's nightmare.

It is imperative that you do nothing when aphids first appear on your roses. Spraying at this stage, even with soap or similar nontoxic substances, is a tragic mistake, for the ladybug's eggs or larvae, as well as other predators, will be killed. You must grit your teeth and bear them for a while. After two weeks or so you should begin to see the small ladybug larvae at work and will notice colonies of aphids reduced to empty white husks. Once the ladybugs establish a presence, the aphids will be kept to minimal levels. If your roses are growing in a light sandy soil, you may find that ants are protecting aphids from predators. This can be alleviated by spreading a thick layer of mulch in the garden. Ants prefer dry, well-drained conditions; under a mulch there is a great deal of moisture, and the ants will not be encouraged to build their colonies.

If you are raising roses in a greenhouse, where ladybugs cannot enter, you have several options. It is possible to buy predators from companies that specialize in biological controls. Another simple but effective control is to hose plants down regularly with a well-directed and strong stream of water. Insecticidal soap can also be effective against aphids, and may be necessary in the greenhouse, where normal insect relationships are disrupted.

Roses vary tremendously in their attractiveness to aphids. One hardy old favorite, F.J. Grootendorst, is notorious as a gourmet treat for aphids. At the nursery we used to spray this variety often to try to keep the aphid population down, with only limited success. Once we let the predators do our work, we found that, after the required waiting period, our Grootendorst becomes a wonderful place to study predators in action. Now our Grootendorsts stay relatively clean all season. In contrast, a new variety, Champlain, must be last on the aphid's list of restaurants, because we never see the pests on this rose.

GALL WASPS

Gall wasps are tiny insects, usually black or orange. They are so small that a hand lens is necessary to see them well, and they are usually noticed only when the gall forms around the larval stage. The galls interfere with the flow of water and nutrients to the sections of stems above them, and occasionally large numbers of galls are noticeable. Where no control is practiced, infestations can build up to levels that can seriously reduce the vigor of your roses.

In the spring, adult wasps lay their eggs in the stem of the rose. These eggs hatch in approximately four days. Once the larvae begin feeding, the plant reacts by producing masses of tissue around the larvae. The larvae overwinter in these protective galls. In spring they pupate. When their host plants are at the proper stage, the adult wasps eat holes through the sides of the galls, emerge, then lay their eggs to begin the new generation.

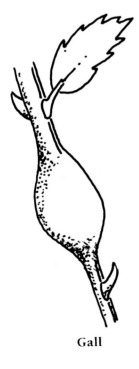

Gall

Gall wasps are seldom a severe problem. To control them, remove the galls as soon as you notice them. If you cut the gall in half with a knife, you will be able to see the larvae inside. Bury or burn the removed galls to ensure there is no threat from another generation. If you keep an eye out, you will notice galls on oak trees, goldenrod and other plants. Each species of gall wasp is specific to a certain species of plant, another testament to the immense diversity of insect life.

LEAFHOPPERS

Leafhopper

Leafhoppers are small, pale green to greenish white and very active creatures that eat foliage with sucking mouthparts. They are found on the undersides of leaves. Through a hand lens, they appear to have a large head with a somewhat triangular body, the wings coming to a high ridge along their backs. Although they are not usually a serious problem on roses, they can reduce the vigor of badly infested plants.

Leafhoppers overwinter both in the egg stage and as adults. Adults become active early in spring and often mate even before leaves appear. They push their eggs into the midrib of the leaves. The first generation appears about the time leaves become full-size, and they begin feeding by sucking sap from the undersides of the leaves. If disturbed, they will live up to their name and hop from leaf to leaf. If an infested plant is shaken, a small cloud of leafhoppers will be airborne, but they settle quickly, as they are not flyers. Several generations are produced each year, and as each leafhopper grows, it sheds its skin in the molting process. These small white skins cling to the undersides of the leaves, confirming the presence of leafhoppers.

Leafhopper populations vary from year to year. The best general advice for leafhoppers is to keep your plants actively growing. They have little effect on a well-fed, well-watered rose.

MITES

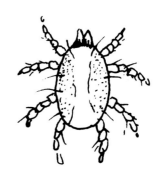

Mite

Mites are closely related to spiders. Several types can infest roses. The most common in northern gardens is the European red mite. The two-spotted mite and the spider mite can be pests in the greenhouse. Mites are quite small and you'll need a hand lens to see them. Their presence is indicated by a general yellowing of the leaves and fine web structures on the undersides of the leaves, where they feed. They are sucking insects that destroy the inside tissues of leaves.

Mites spend the winter as small red eggs on branches, around bud scars or in crevices. About the time apple blossoms are opening, the eggs hatch and the first generation begins to feed. If conditions are right, the mites will begin to multiply rapidly. Their entire life cycle can take as little as four days to complete and several generations a year may occur, although the northern gardener is blessed with a shorter, cooler growing season, which helps to limit the number of generations.

Mites can be thought of as a signal that your roses are not receiving enough water. A well-watered, vigorous rose is rarely affected by mites. Mulching roses will go a long way toward ensuring that your soil stays adequately moist. If the weather is extraordinarily dry, be sure to give your roses a good soaking. If you notice a buildup of mites, wash the foliage. Once off the leaf, mites cannot regain their place on the plant. Mites have numerous predators. Certain species of thrips have a voracious appetite for mites. They eat both the eggs and the larvae. There are also predator mites, which feed on the pest mites. Ladybugs and related insects also enjoy a good meal of mites.

One last note concerns dormant oil. This product can be sprayed on the dormant bush and will smother mite eggs during the early spring. The problem with dormant oil is that it also kills the eggs of predatory mites.

SAWFLIES

Larva of sawfly

Several species of sawfly eat roses. Sawflies are in the larval or caterpillar stage when they do their damage. They are smallish, usually about 1/2 in. (1.3 cm) long, somewhat enlarged at the front and have a characteristic habit when active of holding on to the leaf with their front feet and curling the remainder of their bodies into the air. When resting they remain curled on the underside of the leaf. Some sawflies roll the leaves as they eat them. Others eat all the leaf except the main veins. Populations vary from year to year, but, when dense, sawflies can cause a great deal of damage to rose foliage and are one of the most aggravating pests.

The adult sawfly lays its eggs on the leaves. These hatch out into tiny larvae, which begin feeding immediately. When they reach maturity the larvae fall to the ground, where they spin cocoons around themselves, remaining in the leaf litter until spring, when they emerge with wings and lay eggs to begin the cycle again.

Populations vary so much from year to year that some years sawflies may be no problem at all, while in other years they may strip whole bushes clean. Certain varieties of rose seem to attract sawflies more than others, but no good study on variety susceptibility has been done, to my knowledge. At the first sign of infestation, a thorough hand picking should be done. The more sawflies you pick, the fewer will get a chance to reproduce. A simple but effective technique of lowering sawfly populations is to beat infected rose bushes with a padded stick or to kick them. The caterpillars will drop to the ground. There, away from their habitat, they become easy prey for ground-patrolling birds and insects. Severe infestations can be treated with materials such as rotenone, pyrethrins or insecticidal soap. However, use these as a last resort, as they will disrupt other insect populations. If you have a severe infestation, it would be a good idea to work the soil around the roses deeply or add a thick layer of mulch; this will kill many of the overwintering cocoons by burying them in damp soil. Birds should be encouraged, as they are one of the primary predators of the sawfly.

SPITTLE BUGS

Spittle bugs are also known as froghoppers. They are usually noticeable only when they surround themselves with a protective layer of white foam, which looks just like spit. They have sucking mouthparts that draw sap from the stems of many plants, including roses.

They begin life as eggs, which hatch into small green nymphs. During the year they molt, gaining size as they do so. Eventually they mate and lay eggs in the fall for next year's generation.

Although noticeable, spittle bugs do little harm to roses. Occasionally a larger than normal number may appear on bushes, but these can be easily sprayed off with a garden hose or picked off by hand. I find them interesting and inoffensive and rarely take the time to destroy them.

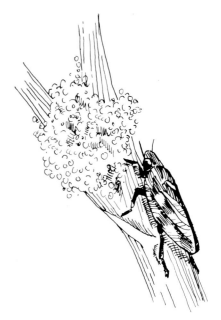

Spittle bug

OTHER PESTS

There are many other insects that attack roses, such as Japanese beetles, chafer beetles and earwigs. Patrol your roses and learn to recognize the presence of such pests. Usually a hand picking will take care of an infestation if caught early. The earwig, a nocturnal species, can be caught in traps made of strips of corrugated cardboard. They crawl into the corrugation at daybreak and can then be disposed of. Solutions to pest problems are often simple. Both the expert and your neighbor may have answers. Magazines and gardening books are mines of information. And remember, if you look with open eyes you may find your own solutions.

DISEASES OF ROSES

Roses have a reputation as troublesome plants that need to be constantly coated with various fungicides to prevent the diseases to which they are prone. In part, this reputation is deserved. Many roses, particularly in the more humid climates, fall victim to rusts, mildews and that most ubiquitous of rose diseases, blackspot. The modern hybrid teas and floribundas are quite susceptible to fungal diseases. The popularity of the hybrid teas, coupled with this weakness, has helped to give the rose its reputation as a difficult subject. The northern rose grower should take heart, however. A good percentage of the super-hardy roses are bred from the more healthy species. With careful planning, you can choose roses that will require little, if any, protection from diseases. At the same time, there are hardy roses that, though prone to some diseases, are so lovely that we cannot bring ourselves to garden without them. So a little advice is in order.

In general fungi, which are among the more serious diseases, are spread in damp conditions. While it is impossible for you to change the weather, you can help discourage fungus. The placement of roses is so important. If your roses are placed in a garden where there is very little air movement, they will take much longer to dry after a rain and will tend to hold the humidity around them. Roses placed where there is good air movement will dry out more quickly and will, therefore, have drier foliage. This will often make the difference between a heavy infestation of fungal disease and a light occurrence or even total absence of disease. Sunlight helps to inhibit fungal growth, and the availability of sun is of great importance in preventing it. Pruning roses to open up the bush will increase both air movement and sunshine within the bush.

Rose varieties differ dramatically in their resistance, or lack of resistance, to disease. If you want to stay away from fungicides, you would be well advised to choose varieties with disease resistance in mind. The descriptions and lists at the back of this book will aid you in this choice.

Cleanliness is crucial in the garden. Be sure to clean up old prunings and any dead branches. Dead branches and stubs left by careless pruning techniques often give diseases like cankers a place to take hold. From there they can move into living tissue, where they can cause severe damage.

BLACKSPOT

Without a doubt, blackspot is the most common scourge of roses. Most varieties are at least partially susceptible, and some varieties can become defoliated if it is not controlled. As its name suggests, the symptoms are black or brown spots, which begin to appear in early summer. The previous year's infected leaves release millions of spores into the air, which settle on the leaves and begin to grow. Blackspot generally shows up first on the older, lower leaves, and can eventually infect the entire shrub.

It is helpful to remove and burn or compost any infected foliage on or under your rose bushes. This will reduce the number of spores the next season. A new layer of mulch each fall will bury overwintering spores and prevent them from dispersing. Keep susceptible varieties pruned to an open shape and try to get as much air movement as possible around the plants. Peter Beales, in his book *Classic Roses*, recommends as a preventive measure using overhead sprinklers every ten days at night for periods of at least five hours. The continual washing removes many of the spores from the leaf surface. Although I have not tried this, it may be worthwhile. If you wish to grow some of the more susceptible varieties, you will need to begin a preventive spray program in mid-spring. Wettable sulfur powder provides reasonably good protection and does not have the toxicity of fungicides such as Captan or Benlate, although it does not have the residual property of these fungicides. Spray after each rain or wet period. Use a few drops of a liquid soap in your sprayer to help spread the sulfur evenly over the foliage. Without a spreader the sulfur will tend to bead and roll off the leaves. An old remedy uses baking soda (sodium bicarbonate) as a preventive spray. Mix 1 oz. (30 g) of baking soda in 10 gallons (40 L) of water and apply after damp periods. I assume the baking soda changes the acidity of the leaf surface, making it an inhospitable place for fungi to grow.

Some wonderful breeding work has been done in the past fifty years to develop blackspot resistance. Some of the most important work has been carried out by Wilhelm Kordes of Germany. Using a particularly resistant seedling, Kordes has bred numerous varieties, including some reasonably hardy modern shrub types, which are quite resistant to blackspot. Felicitas Svejda of Canada has also concentrated much of her efforts on disease resistance, and the results, called the Explorer Series, are nearly all resistant to blackspot. *Rosa rugosa* is a species commonly used in the breeding of hardy roses and is one of the most resistant to blackspot.

CANKER

Cankers usually appear as the result of poor sanitation and pruning. The cankers show up as brown or orange spots on dead wood and then spread to the adjacent live wood. By pruning out dead wood, canker can be almost wholly prevented. Use sharp pruning shears that will not tear wood, and cut cleanly and closely to the nearest live branch. Burn canker when it is found or put it in an actively working compost pile.

CROWN GALL

Crown gall is found on the roots of roses and related plants. It is caused by a bacterium (a microscopic one-celled organism) that is found in nearly all soils and that gains entrance through a mechanical injury or insect damage. The galls are irregular, bulbous growths, which over time can become quite large. There is some debate over how much crown gall harms the plants it infects, but the concensus is that it does affect the vigor and longevity of the plant. Do not use gall-infected plants if you can avoid it. If for some reason you have to use a plant that shows galls, cut off the infected root. A biological control for crown gall is now available. Before planting, the roots are dipped into a solution of water and a bacterium (*Agrobacterium radiobacter*), which inhibits the growth of the crown gall bacterium. This specific bacterium is quite safe to use.

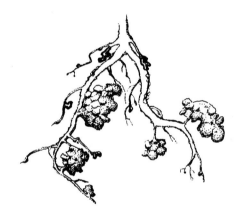

Crown gall is a bacterial infection of roses present in most soils. The bacteria enter through wounds in the roots caused by mechanical or insect injury.

POWDERY MILDEW

Powdery mildew shows up as a grayish-white coating on the surface of infected leaves. It is particularly troublesome in late summer. Susceptible varieties can be severely harmed unless measures are taken.

Mildew, as is the case with so many diseases, tends to show up on stressed plants more than on healthy ones. Roses that are either poorly nourished or overstimulated by heavy feeding of nitrogen fertilizers are particularly prone to mildew. Plants that do not receive enough water are likewise affected. Keep your plant mulched and well fed with compost. This will promote a balanced growth that will help to prevent mildew. Place susceptible varieties in areas where they will get good air circulation. If you are growing a particularly susceptible variety, you may find it necessary to adopt a spray program using wettable sulfur. Bicarbonate of soda can be used as well.

ROSE MIDGE

The rose midge is one of the most frustrating of rose pests. The adult midge is a very small, yellowish fly that lays its eggs in the stem just below a forming bud. When the egg hatches, the tiny larva begins feeding. As it feeds, it disrupts the flow of nutrients and water to that side of the bud on which it is feeding. The result is that the bud bends to one side. The lack of food and water is usually fatal to the bud, and it blackens and dies before opening. Careful and consistent examination of your roses is critical to keeping this insect at bay. Any stems that show the characteristic bent bud should be removed immediately and destroyed. This will disrupt the cycle and prevent further generations from developing. Diligence is the gardener's best weapon against this pest.

RUST

Rust shows up as orange patches on the undersides of leaves and can, if unchecked, spread to the stems. It shows up in warm, moist weather. It does not seem to be as widespread in the more northern areas. This may reflect a difference in the types of roses grown, or perhaps rust is unable to overwinter in colder temperatures.

The life cycle of rust is much the same as that of blackspot, over-wintering on leaves. If you notice rust, immediately remove and burn any infected foliage. Infected leaves should likewise be removed from the ground to prevent re-infection. A new layer of mulch will help prevent dropped leaves from dispersing spores into the air.

VIRUSES

Viruses are mysterious organisms that show up throughout the animal and plant world. Virus-infected roses will show symptoms such as yellowed and streaked leaves. The flowers may tend to be small and few, and foliage may drop prematurely. You cannot cure virus. It is most often spread when infected stock is used for nursery propagation. If you are sure you have a virus-infected rose, and not simply a rose that is suffering from pests, lack of water or nutritional deficiencies, rip it out. Sucking insects such as aphids can spread a virus to healthy plants.

Reading through a section on insects and diseases can be disheartening. Please, do not be discouraged. Our gardens are never sprayed (with the possible exception of a little sulfur on a few blackspot-susceptible varieties), and we have no serious problems. Keep your garden well tended, spend time building healthy soil, choose healthy varieties where possible, and you will be rewarded with healthy roses.

5

Propagation

ROSE PETALS LITTERED ACROSS THE FLOOR AND THE GENTLE click of pruning shears are some of the sights and sounds that surround me when working at my favorite pastime – propagation. The creation of new plants is one of the great pleasures of the horticultural world and is for me the primary reason for being a nurseryman. Propagation lies at the very base of horticulture. Whether from seed, cuttings, grafting or budding, the result is the same – a new generation of plants. Through centuries of trial and error, propagators have discovered the easiest ways to produce the many plants that gardeners have been interested in growing. A great deal of effort has been devoted to the rose.

Several methods of propagation are used. Each method has its own merits and problems. Some methods work for some roses and not for others. The problem of growing roses in the north throws a curve into the equation, and it is my contention that getting hardy roses on their own roots is a decided advantage. Be that as it may, all the methods described below can be successfully used to produce roses.

If you are curious about how roses are produced, or if you are interested in producing your own plants, the following section describes the various techniques in some detail. If you are not interested in the actual propagation procedures, please feel free to skip this section.

Propagating new plants is one of the pleasures of gardening.

SEEDS

Growing roses from seeds is the oldest form of propagation. As the petals of a rose unfold, the female part of the flower – the pistil – becomes receptive to fertilization by the male pollen. Usually this fertilization occurs between two plants; therefore the seed contains characteristics of both parents and is unique. These differences are usually minor within a species, although occasionally a seedling will differ substantially from the general type.

If you would like to try growing roses from seeds, collect them in the fall when the hips are fully ripe. Test for ripeness by opening the hip. The seeds inside should be turning a deep tan to brown. Immature seeds will appear whitish or very light tan. Once collected, rose seeds, particularly from hardy species, will require a period of cool, damp conditions called stratification. Seed can be planted directly into prepared earth beds or trays in the fall. If you use trays, put these in a place where they will remain near the freezing point till spring. Be sure they are protected from mice, which will make short work of your seeds. Another method is to mix l part seed to at least 3 parts of a barely damp, sterile medium such as peat moss. Place the mix into a sealed polyethylene bag. Put this in a refrigerator and keep just above freezing for three or four months. Be careful not to keep fruit in the same refrigerator, as stored fruit gives off ethylene gas, which may injure the seed. Germination should be prompt in warmer temperatures.

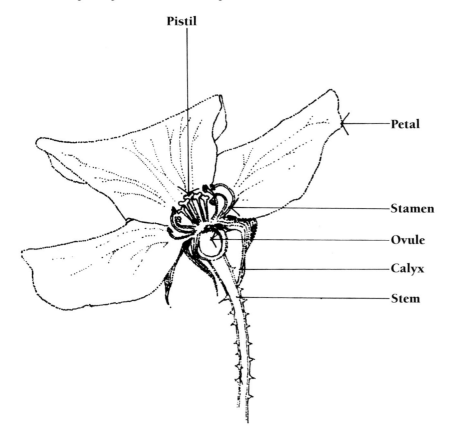

Pistil

Petal

Stamen

Ovule

Calyx

Stem

The petals of a rose attract insects, which transfer pollen formed in sacs at the tips of the stamens to the pistils. Growing through the pistil, the pollen enters the ovule, where fertilization and seed formation take place.

Seeds collected from any rose will produce seedlings that are different from the parent. For this reason, seeds are generally used only for the propagation of species roses and in breeding work.

Rose breeders have a curious but fascinating job. By crossing two varieties with desirable characteristics, they try to create different roses. The technique of breeding is simple, but proper timing and delicate hand work are needed to ensure good results.

To cross two roses, first choose the female or seed parent. This parent must be a fertile variety. Fertile roses form fruit (rosehips). Carefully remove all the petals from the flowers of your seed parent just as they begin to open. With tweezers, gently remove the tops of the stamens, which contain the pollen. Put a paper bag over these emasculated flowers for approximately 24 hours to prevent unwanted pollen from fertilizing them, then examine the pistils of these flowers. When they are slightly sticky, they are receptive. Take pollen which you have gathered from your male parent's stamens and gently brush it on the pistils of the female parent. This is usually done with a fine sable brush. If you are using several different male parents be sure to carefully wash out the brush with alcohol and dry thoroughly each time you change pollen sources. Cover the flower with the paper bag again. After a week or two the fruit will begin to swell if fertilization has been successful. Remove the bags and carefully mark each cluster, noting the male parent used for the cross. Harvest the seed in fall when the fruit turns color. Check to be sure the seeds have turned to a tan or brown color. Unripe seed will be white. Most seedlings you produce will probably be roses of little value, but the dream of creating that special new rose keeps the breeder ever hopeful.

Although few people have the patience for breeding roses, and even fewer have the time and money required for a major breeding program, innumerable varieties have been created by enthusiastic amateurs. Even if you do not create the rose of the century, the process and results can be satisfaction in themselves.

LAYERING

As a rose bush grows, it often sends out underground stems or suckers. By digging these suckers out and cutting them off from the main plant, you can easily create new plants. Among the northern roses, *Rosa rugosa* is well known for its suckering nature, and these suckers are a simple way to produce a few plants from the original. Be careful when taking suckers from a budded or grafted plant. The rootstock will be totally different from the variety on top. A careful examination of the leaves will usually show any differences. Even if a variety does not readily produce suckers, however, the process of layering offers an opportunity to the propagator.

Layering involves bending down a stem and burying it several inches into the soil with the tip protruding. A metal or wooden stake may be required to keep the layer from popping out of the ground. Be sure to keep the layer well covered and damp. Some propagators wound the base

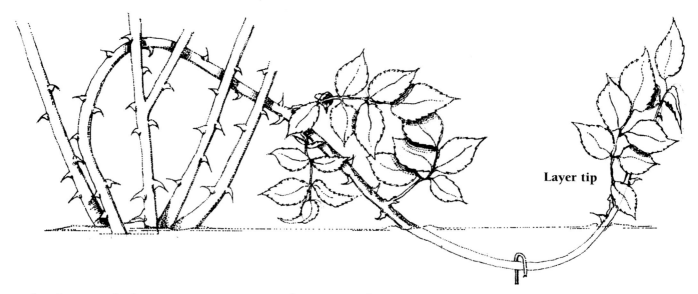

Layer tip

before burying the layer to promote root production. Hard-to-root varieties may also benefit from the application of a rooting hormone such as IBA (indole-3-butyric acid) to the wound.

The buried portion will eventually form roots. If layered in the spring, most layers will have formed enough roots so you can remove them by the fall or early the next spring. A few varieties may require longer periods. When digging these layers be careful not to injure the delicate new roots. To remove from the parent plant, cut the base of the layer cleanly off with snips, and if the top is long, cut it back to only a few buds. Plant and water well.

This technique is easy and reliable, particularly for the home gardener, as it takes no special equipment or structures. The commercial grower faces the problem of producing large numbers of plants. To accomplish this, many growers bud their roses.

Burying a stem underground stimulates roots to form. Later the layer tip, with its new roots, can be severed from the mother plant and planted.

BUDDING

Budding is the preferred technique of most commercial growers. Although it requires some practice to master the art of budding, it is essentially a simple process and can easily be performed by anyone with enough interest and a sharp knife.

Budding is the placing of a bud from the desired variety onto a rootstock. Several rootstocks are in general use today, though most growers in Europe and North America use either *Rosa multiflora* or *Rosa canina*. Thornless varieties of these species are preferred.

The rootstocks are grown for one or two years either in the field or in containers. Budding is usually performed during the period of active growth, which in most northern areas is between late June and mid-August. Prepare the rootstocks by cleaning off any adhering soil. With a sharp, thin-bladed knife, make a T-shaped incision 1 to 2 in. (2.5 to 5 cm) from the soil line; the cuts should slice through the bark, no deeper. Pry back the two corner flaps to insert the bud.

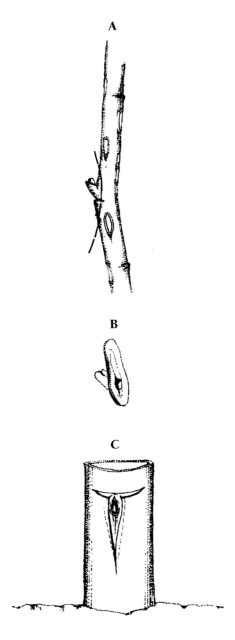

Budding
A Removing a bud of the desired variety.
B The shield bud with inner wood removed ready to insert.
C The bud inserted under the bark ready to be tied in place.

Single buds of the desired variety are cut from stems that are nearly ready to flower. The cut is made just slightly into the woody portion of the stem; the resultant shape is somewhat shield-like. Carefully remove the woody portion under the bud so that only the bark and the bud itself remain. Insert the bud, pointing naturally upward, into the incision.

After positioning, bind the bud to the rootstock by wrapping around it an elastic band or a latex tie especially made for the purpose. This wrapping ensures that there is good contact between the bud and rootstock and prevents air from getting into the wound and drying out the bud before it has a chance to unite with the stock. After a month, remove these ties and examine the bud. If it has taken it will be green and swollen. If not, it will be blackened and dead. Leave the successful plants until either winter or, preferably in colder areas, very early spring, before cutting off the tops of the stocks 3/8 in. (1 cm) above the bud. This cut should slope slightly down and away from the bud. As the bud grows, rub off any suckers from the rootstock. If not removed, these may use up much of the plant's strength.

Budding has several advantages. The use of an established rootstock furnishes the bud with tremendous vigor, and a sizable plant can be produced in a single year. The use of rootstocks also imparts vigor into varieties that, on their own roots, would remain smaller. Perhaps the major advantage, from the nurseryman's point of view, is that a plant can be produced from a single bud. This means that the required number of stock plants, from which the buds are taken, is relatively small.

There are disadvantages as well. A budded plant remains two separate plants. The rootstock is quite different from the top variety. Often the rootstock will send up suckers. The flowers on these suckers will be completely different. A double red rose suddenly has small single white flowers in its midst. Gardeners not familiar with how roses are produced often say, "My rose has gone wild." Though the flowers may be pretty, most gardeners do not want the rootstock suckers, and removing them is a constant problem that must be attended to with budded roses. A second disadvantage is a more serious problem, particularly for growers living in hardiness Zone 4 and colder. The most common rose rootstocks are not reliably hardy that far north. Even though the variety may be perfectly hardy, you may lose your plant if the rootstock suffers winterkill. Without an insulating layer of snow, frost penetrates deeply into the ground and temperatures may fall below what the rootstock can tolerate. This is especially troublesome in areas that do not receive reliable snowcover.

Plant budded roses so that the bud union is a good 2 to 4 in. (5 to 10 cm) below the soil surface. This will prevent light, which will initiate suckering, from reaching the rootstock. As well, it will give the variety a chance to form roots of its own, thereby making the plant less dependent upon the survival of the rootstock. In heavier clay soils, planting deeply may at first reduce the rose's vigor because oxygen levels will be lower, but as roots form on the upper sections, vigor will return. Plants that are pruned heavily will tend to sucker more. The reduction of the top stimulates dormant buds on the rootstock into growth to try to replace the lost leaf area. A gentler pruning regime on budded roses may therefore be advantageous.

GRAFTING

Grafting and budding accomplish the same task. Only the technique differs. Instead of placing a bud under the bark, a section of stem is placed on top of the rootstock.

Grafting is usually done on dormant rootstocks in winter or very early spring. Several different methods are used to join the variety to the rootstock. The most commonly used are the splice graft or, alternatively, the whip-and-tongue graft.

Two things are absolutely necessary to the success of grafting. You must have a razor-sharp, thin-bladed knife and tough fingers. Rose thorns are difficult to deal with at the best of times, but they can be a real nuisance when you're grafting. I find it extremely difficult to graft with gloves on. Grafting requires dexterity, and gloves just get in the way. However, if you have thin leather gloves, you may find them useful. Many rose varieties have thorns that are easily removed by gently pressing them sideways. Your job will be much easier with such roses.

To make a whip-and-tongue graft, cut the rootstock with a sharp blade just above the roots at an angle that leaves the length of the exposed surface about three times the diameter of the stock. Halfway down the cut, and with the blade pointing down the slope, make a second cut. When making this cut raise the blade just slightly from the surface, so that a thin flap is created. This cut should be no longer than one-quarter the length of the exposed surface of the initial cut. Using a section of stem containing one to five buds, make the same sequence of cuts on the bottom of the piece from the desired variety. This piece is referred to as the scion. Slide the scion down onto the rootstock. The thin flaps at the center of each cut should lock the two pieces. Fit them gently and snugly together. If the cuts are flat and the flaps are thin, there should be good surface-to-surface contact. When you fit the graft, it is essential that at least one side of the union have the cambiums aligned. (The cambium is the thin green layer just under the bark.) This is where cell division occurs and therefore where the two sections will knit together. Without proper alignment, the cells will not be able to connect, and the graft will fail. If the scion and rootstock are different sizes, make certain at least one side is aligned.

Once you have locked the two pieces together, bind them tightly with a budding rubber, masking tape or even string. When tying, be careful not to shift the alignment. Once tied, brush on a grafting wax to seal the graft. This will prevent the graft from drying out before healing takes place. Several grafting waxes are available on the market. If you are unable to find a commercial preparation, melted paraffin wax will work. We make up our own mix of 1 part rosin to 2 parts beeswax. This must be heated to be workable. (Rosin, which is the hardened gum of

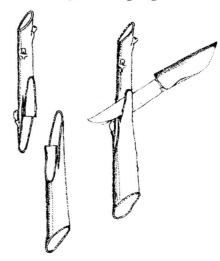

Whip-and-tongue graft

Healthy material, a sharp knife to make flat, clean cuts, and good alignment of the inner bark (cambium) are the essential elements of successful grafting.

Wedge graft

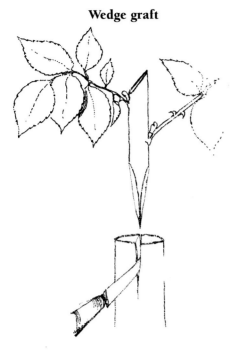

A simple and effective method of grafting, particularly on small material in the greenhouse.

certain pines, is becoming increasingly difficult to find.) Place your grafts in a cool place until you are ready to plant. Be sure that the roots are kept slightly moist.

There is a variation of the grafting process that we have found very useful. This technique is used in the greenhouse, but could be adapted to a coldframe or humidity tent. We collect sticks of both the desired rootstock and the variety in late spring and summer. Only slightly hardened, new wood is used, and this should be vigorous and reasonably thick. First remove the leaves from the rootstock sticks. Cut these sticks into sections 3-4 in. (8-10 cm) long, being sure to keep track of which ends are top and which bottom. Using a sharp knife, make a vertical cut down into the center of the top of a rootstock section. This cut should only be 1/2 in. (1.3 cm) deep. Next cut a section of the variety stick, leaving 2 or 3 leaves on each section. Slice the base of the variety section into a 3/4 in. (2 cm) long wedge. Using the tip of the knife to open the top of the rootstock section slightly, insert the wedged end of the variety into the cut, aligning the cambium layers as you do so. Push the wedge far enough so that it is snug, but not so far that it will split the rootstock section. If properly made, the graft will be snug enough without needing to be tied.

Dip the base of the completed graft into a rooting hormone. We usually use a 0.2% IBA talc powder preparation, but a similar-strength liquid hormone will work. Gently stick the cutting into a rooting medium, which should be clean and perfectly drained. A mixture of 4 parts perlite to 1 part peat works well. Clean sharp sand will work as well. If kept sufficiently moist and warm, this grafted cutting will root within two or three weeks. Once rooted it can be potted up until it is sufficiently acclimatized to be planted outdoors.

Grafting is a reasonably simple and rewarding technique for producing roses. Like budding, it creates plants that are the union of two different varieties, and the problems of suckering and rootstock hardiness are the same. On the whole, grafting is somewhat more reliable than budding when done on rootstocks growing in the field. Newly budded roses can suffer winterkill in areas with very low winter temperatures, especially when there is no snowcover. Grafting is one of the oldest propagating methods for roses, and it is still one of the most dependable.

CUTTINGS

Nearly all varieties of roses can be rooted from cuttings. Some are easy to root, while others are difficult. Most fall in the middle. Yet this simple technique is rarely used by commercial growers because budding and grafting methods are more economically advantageous.

There are two general types of cuttings – softwood and hardwood. The names refer to the condition of the wood when the cuttings are taken. Softwood cuttings are taken in spring and summer, when the wood is actively growing and fairly soft. Hardwood cuttings are taken when the plants are dormant and the wood is quite firm. The vast majority of rose cuttings are softwood. It is my experience that hardwood cutting propagation in the north is usually unsuccessful. In England, where winter temperatures are mild, hardwood cuttings are stuck directly in the ground and usually root by spring. In our cold winters, this technique usually fails, and we confine our work to softwood cuttings. The process of rooting rose cuttings is quite simple. What is needed is an understanding of the environmental requirements necessary to keep the cutting healthy until it is ready to be put out as a rooted plant.

Collect softwood cuttings as soon as the first flower buds form in the late spring or early summer. Cuttings taken from stems that are just about to flower consistently have the highest percentage of rooting. Gather your cuttings when conditions are cool. Morning is a good time, as the stems have not been wilted by the sun. Never let cuttings dry out. Move them quickly into a cool place and sprinkle with water immediately.

Take great care in selecting your cuttings. You will not succeed without healthy cuttings. Cuttings should be collected from well-fed, actively growing and disease-free plants. A healthy cutting has an adequate supply of nutrients in its tissues to sustain it until it roots. Diseases or insects can interfere with the cutting's ability to function properly. Cuttings with insects such as aphids on them can cause havoc in the greenhouse. We soak all cuttings for a few minutes in an insecticidal soap dip before rinsing them. Insecticidal soaps are nontoxic to mammals but kill most insects in short order.

The availability of material and the number of plants you want to produce determine how large a cutting you take. Most roses will form roots on small cuttings with only one or two leaves. If material is available though, larger cuttings are preferable. A cutting 4 to 8 in. (10 to 20 cm) long will make a much stronger plant than a smaller cutting. Cut any flowers or flower buds off the tips. While the cut is still fresh, dip the base of the cuttings in rooting hormone. When using talc preparations of rooting hormone, be sure to dip only the very bottom of the cuttings in the hormone and shake off any excess. Too much hormone can burn them. When using liquid hormone preparations, be sure to dip the base only for as long as recommended. Softwood rose cuttings do not require a strong hormone concentration. Use a 0.2% IBA preparation (#2). Stronger concentrations can burn the cutting.

Stick the cuttings in a rooting medium. A rooting medium serves two purposes. It holds the cutting in place and provides enough moisture around the base to aid the rooting process. An excess of moisture, however, can cause the base to rot. The ideal medium, therefore, has perfect drainage yet holds enough water to keep the cutting moist. I have found that a mixture of 4 parts perlite to 1 part peat moss works well. Most references I have read recommend 1 part perlite or sand to 1 part peat. Our experiences with rooting mediums like these were disastrous. We lost crop after crop from rot. We gradually decreased the peat content until we arrived at the 4 to 1 mix. The roses will root in straight perlite, but once roots form they seem to need some organic material to toughen up. Roots grown in straight perlite do not seem to survive transplanting as well as roots grown in a perlite-peat mixture. Although perlite is an ideal material, if you cannot obtain it, use clean sand. Sand has been the material of choice for centuries. Just be sure it has no organic residues. These organics harbor pathogens, which can cause rotting.

A great deal has been written about the use of fertilizers in rooting mediums. The rooting medium itself is sterile; therefore, when the cutting roots there are no nutrients to absorb, and the cutting essentially feeds off itself. Organic fertilizers such as compost present problems when used in rooting mediums, for they can contain life forms that may feed on the injured portions of the cutting and may eventually rot it. It would seem that fertilizer added to the medium might help to feed the cutting until it can be potted up in a soil mix. However, free nitrogen in the medium before the cutting has rooted promotes the growth of a range of microscopic life forms, some of which will feed on the injured tissues at the base of the cutting and increase the likelihood of rot.

The compromise we have adopted is to use a slow-release form of fertilizer that is activated by moisture and temperature. These fertilizers are made of granules coated by a thin layer that releases the nutrients gradually throughout the growing season. Although not as readily available as the more common fertilizers, slow-release fertilizers can be found in many garden centers and nurseries.

When mixed in small quantities in the rooting medium, a slow-release fertilizer can be very beneficial. When the cuttings are first stuck, the coating around the individual grains of fertilizer prevents any appreciable amount of nutrient from escaping into the medium. When the first roots appear after about two weeks, the levels of fertilizer are sufficient to provide nutrients to the new roots. Before we began using this slow-release formula, many of our cuttings would form roots, then drop their leaves and die. The use of a slow-release fertilizer prevents this, and the cuttings are able to begin growth as soon as roots emerge.

Creating the proper environment for cuttings is critical to the success of the whole operation. What the propagator needs to achieve is a humidity level that is high enough to prevent the cutting from wilting yet not so wet that it will saturate the rooting medium and leach out nutrients from the leaves. Several innovations in propagation equipment have provided commercial growers with systems that create a fog or fog-like environment in the greenhouse. These systems spray a very fine mist that floats in the air and surrounds the cuttings with moisture without soaking the cuttings and medium. The older type of overhead mist nozzles use more water and tend to keep the cuttings so wet that they run with water. This system can be used with success, but it is not as desirable.

Most gardeners do not have fancy systems or greenhouses in which to propagate their cuttings. There is a simple alternative. A small cold-frame structure built on the north side of a building can be a useful propagating facility. By placing it on the north side, it will not receive direct sun, which can heat up the interior and raise temperatures to dangerous levels, thereby drying out the cuttings. During the daylight hours, keep the cuttings slightly damp by occasionally spraying with a hose or a simple set of built-in nozzles. If the coldframe is tight, the humidity can be kept high with only a few mistings a day. Hot days may require more mistings. Once cuttings begin to root, the top of the coldframe can gradually be raised for short periods until the cuttings become acclimated to the drier atmosphere, at which point they can be transplanted.

Temperature is important in determining how speedily your cuttings will root. Reasonably high temperatures will speed the process of cell activity. Once above 88°F (30°C), however, growth slows down. Higher temperatures can be detrimental to the cuttings. Cuttings that have been allowed to dry even for as short a time as 15 minutes may be irreparably damaged. This is why many amateur propagators fail in their attempts to root roses. The process is simple, but constant vigilance is necessary to succeed.

Heat from below can also be an advantage when rooting cuttings. This heat can be provided by hot water pipes or electric resistance cable run in the bed under the cuttings. A constant temperature of 70-77°F (22-25°C) is ideal. We have found that *Rosa rugosa* hybrids respond well to bottom heat, particularly when cuttings are taken early in the growing season.

Once the cuttings have produced several strong roots they should be potted. Move your newly transplanted roses into an area where you can water frequently to help the new plants gradually adjust to the drier atmosphere. Many plants are lost at this stage, and nothing hurts more than to have gone through all the trials of rooting your cuttings only to see them dry up after transplanting. It is also a good idea to partially shade your newly rooted plants to keep temperatures from becoming too high and drying out the leaves. At this point the leaves are "lazy." On their surfaces are small pores, called stomata, which open and close to regulate the amount of water in the leaves. In the high humidity of a greenhouse or coldframe they seem to grow sluggish and do not respond as rapidly to changes in humidity levels. If the plant is put in the hot sun, the stomata stay open, the moisture in the leaves escapes and they dry up. If given several days of slow adjustment after removal from the greenhouse or coldframe, however, the leaves start functioning normally and are ready to face the harsh realities of sun, wind and heat.

At the nursery these plants are moved out into the field to grow for the remainder of the season and through the next year before they are sold. At home you can plant these young roses in their intended site. Be careful to keep them adequately watered. A mulch will help to ensure they do not dry out. Once firmly established in the soil, the rose will need only routine care.

It is my contention that a rose on its own roots is a superior plant, particularly when placed in a northern garden setting. The aggravating problem of rootstock suckering disappears. The problem of incompatibility between the rootstock and the variety is nonexistent. Most important, you need only worry about the hardiness of the variety. Many of

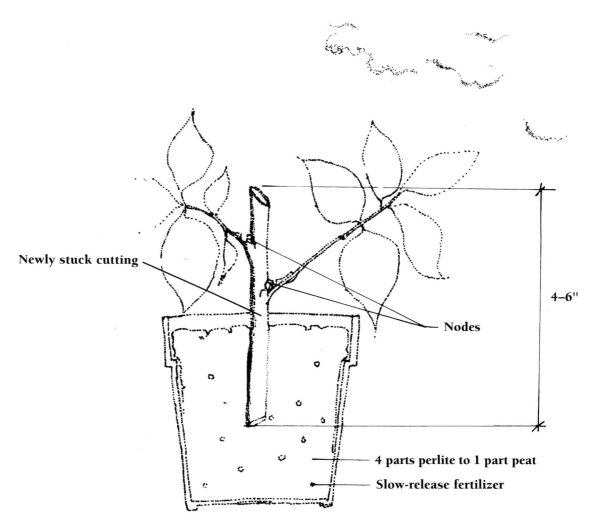

Newly stuck cutting

Nodes

4–6"

4 parts perlite to 1 part peat

Slow-release fertilizer

A well-drained and sterile rooting medium, rooting hormone and high humidity are necessary to root a cutting. It is a simple process, but one requiring unfailing diligence.

the varieties that can be grown in the far north are much hardier than the rootstocks on which they are budded. You are far less likely to lose your rose to winter injury. As well, often the rootstock will influence the hardening off process in the fall. The more tender rootstock will keep the variety growing longer into the fall than it might if it were on its own roots. Another factor that is perhaps overlooked by most rose growers is the rootstock's influence on the variety's vigor. In many cases increased vigor is not an advantage, particularly when you are seeking a rose for a small space. Many dwarf or low-growing roses become far larger plants when pushed by their rootstocks. By propagating roses on their own roots, you can be more certain of their ultimate size. These factors make the time and trouble involved in rooting roses worthwhile.

It is a regrettable fact that roses on their own roots are very difficult to find in the nursery trade. For the northern grower it is worth the search. If you have the inclination and the time, and can put together the facilities, the challenging and rewarding process of rooting roses can let you produce your own. There is no finer feeling than the pleasure of watching the first blossom unfurling on a rose bush that you have helped create.

Dew accentuates the fluid lines of Rheinaupark.

PART II

The Varieties: Petals of Light

**Henry Kelsey is the best red
climbing rose for cold areas.**

6

Climbers

Shrubs growing taller than 6 ft. (1.8 m) and
suitable for tying to supports

AÏCHA

CAPTAIN SAMUEL HOLLAND

HENRY KELSEY

JOHN CABOT

WILLIAM BAFFIN

WILLIAM BOOTH

AÏCHA

Parentage: unknown, Rosa spinosissima hybrid.

For me, this rose symbolizes the exciting new generation of hardy roses. When the first blooms on my plants opened, I was intrigued by their distinctive form and dazzled by their sunshine-yellow color. I would visit the plants every day to watch the newest buds unfurl and the older flowers pale to a delicate pastel.

Each flower's immense outer petals cradle five inner petals, which in turn encircle the largest grouping of stamens I have seen in a rose. Its flowers are borne on vigorous and thorny stems, which can be trained to form a spectacular climber, one that is perfectly happy to spend the winter in the chill wind. Although our plants are young, they have performed so well that I have little hesitation in recommending this rose for northern growers.

This is also an easy rose to grow, with healthy deep green foliage. Aïcha is very difficult to propagate from cuttings and is usually budded or layered. The gently arching stems create an admirably shaped bush if you prefer not to use it as a climber, and those with a nose for fragrance will delight in the perfume of this dazzling newcomer.

You may still have a difficult time finding this new rose, but make the effort. Even on a cloudy day the cheerful petals of Aïcha bring a welcome sunshine into the garden, and you will be amply rewarded for the time spent obtaining it.

CAPTAIN SAMUEL HOLLAND

Parentage: L25 (Rosa kordesii × D07 (Red Dawn × Suzanne)) ×
D25 (Red Dawn × Suzanne).

Captain Samuel Holland charted the coasts of Maritime Canada in the sixteenth century. It is likely that this new rose will become far better known than its namesake. Clusters of tubular buds unfurl to form rounded semi-double flowers of softest red that fade to deep pink. The long, lime-green shoots arch slightly with their own weight, eventually creating an erect bush with great tenacity and vigor. The medium green foliage is rarely touched by blackspot or mildew.

Captain Samuel Holland is a welcome addition to the stable of hardy pillar roses that northern gardeners can use as climbers. Its bud hardiness falls just short of the slightly hardier William Baffin, but not by much. It is a relatively easy rose to root from softwood cuttings. Like many of the hardiest climbers, its fragrance is slight at best, but a Captain Samuel Holland in bloom will be payment in full for the planting, fertilizing and pruning you invest.

HENRY KELSEY

Parentage: Rosa kordesii × *hardy seedling of complex origin.*

Delicate arches hugged by winding branches, clothed in lustrous green foliage and dripping with vivid red roses – Henry Kelsey is a vision of rose heaven.

This recent introduction from Agriculture Canada has long arching canes that can be tied up and used as a climber. If left to grow naturally, Henry Kelsey is a low, arching, somewhat pendulous bush. I have used it as a medium-height ground cover, although it is perhaps a bit sparse for this purpose. When tied up, it makes an admirable climber. A well-grown Henry Kelsey will send up fantastically vigorous long shoots, which in just a few seasons will top an arch or trellis.

Vigor alone makes Henry Kelsey a standout, but the deep red petals, contrasting with the golden yellow stamens, create an irresistible lure. Large clusters appear from early summer until the first frosts. The intense red of the new petals gradually fades to a deep rose as the blooms drop cleanly off the bush.

Henry Kelsey is highly resistant to powdery mildew. Although it is not immune to blackspot, this fungal disease is not a serious threat. This rose can be left on the trellis in Zones 4 and 5 without serious winter injury. It is easy to propagate from softwood cuttings or layering.

Henry Kelsey is the best red climbing rose available for cold areas. It is superior to existing red climbers, and it should be in every collection where such a rose is desired.

JOHN CABOT

Parentage: Rosa kordesii *Wulff* × (*Masquerade* × *Rosa laxa*).

Many years ago I walked up to a display of roses at the Agricultural Research Station near us. I was so enthralled by what I saw that I asked permission to take a few cuttings. Several roses stood out among the many in the group. One in particular, labelled L07, caught my eye. The bush was a powerfully upright yet arching plant covered in symmetrical double blooms that were a deep orchid pink, almost red. Its robust, healthy glow convinced me that here was a rose worth watching. Several years later I read that a new rose called John Cabot had been released, originally grown as seedling L07.

John Cabot has helped to set new standards for hardy roses. Its symmetrical, robust form, coupled with its long blooming season and excellent disease resistance, make it one of the most important new roses for northern gardens. It is also reasonably easy to propagate from softwood cuttings. It is difficult to know whether to call John Cabot a vigorous shrub rose or a climber, because it can be either. Since roses with such vigor and long flowering season are rare, I have decided to include it with the climbers.

WILLIAM BAFFIN

Parentage: open pollinated seedling of L48 (Rosa kordesii Wulff × complex hardy seedling).

One of my favorite pastimes is watching how people react when they walk through the gate of our garden and look out across the multitude of shrubs, perennials, vines and evergreens that lies before them. In the late summer, as many of the roses and daylilies are waning, most eyes are instantly drawn to a corner where a semi-circular hedge of robust rose bushes grows.

Of all the climbers we have grown William Baffin has impressed us most, not only with its strawberry ice cream flowers but also with its vigor and health. As a bush William Baffin is upright and slightly arching, with a dense, full look – perfect for a tall hedge. As a climber it is unmatched. Your only problem may be to keep its vigor from overfilling the trellis with strong, thick canes. You certainly will not have to worry about fussing over this rose. Unless your winter is truly arctic, you will be able to grow William Baffin. We have never seen an injured bud in our garden. And it's healthy – no blackspot, no mildew, no rust – and easy to root from softwood cuttings.

The loose, carefree blooms of William Baffin are charming. They are certainly not aristocratic. If you are looking for a healthy, ironclad hardy, robust rose that is blanketed by clusters of bloom throughout the entire season, this is the rose for you. William Baffin should assume an important place in the northern garden.

WILLIAM BOOTH

Parentage: L83 (Rosa kordesii G49) × A72 (Arthur Bell × Applejack).

The vigor of this rose is truly astounding. New shoots seem to erupt from the ground and soar upward, offering to the sky clusters of slightly cupped single flowers, cherry red in color, with white centers. The simple flowers appear in profusion till fall. The petals often twist and curl inward at the outer edges, an effect somewhat like crepe. The leaves of this energetic climber are dark green with red hues prevailing on the growing tips. Although you may see some leaf spot on older foliage, the beauty of this bush is rarely diminished by disease.

Alas, fragrance is not to be found here, but hardiness, vigor and color compensate. Propagators will find it easy to root. This rose sets hips in profusion. Those wishing for maximum bloom will want to remove the old flower heads to hasten more growth and therefore more bloom. If you love the effect of the once popular single climber American Pillar but need something hardier, you will revel in the sumptuous display provided by William Booth, a treat similar in appearance to the older variety but longer-lasting.

Harison's Yellow is an adaptable rose that survives the frigid temperatures of a northern winter.

7

Tall Shrubs

Shrubs growing up to 6 ft. (1.8 m) or more

ALBA MAXIMA
ALEXANDER MACKENZIE
BLANC DOUBLE DE COUBERT
CARMENETTA
CHLORIS
CONSTANCE SPRY
F.J. GROOTENDORST
WHITE GOOTENDOORST
FRÜHLINGSGOLD
GERANIUM
GOLDBUSCH
HANSA
HARISON'S YELLOW
JOHN DAVIS
MARIE VICTORAN
MRS. ANTHONY WATERER
MME. PLANTIER
QUADRA
ROSAIRIE DE L'HAY
ROBUSTA
SARAH VAN FLEET
SCABROSA
SCHARLACHGLUT
THÉRÈSE BUGNET
WILLIAM LOBB

ALBA MAXIMA

Parentage: unknown, Rosa alba *hybrid.*

Years ago, I was driving through a quiet fishing village marveling at a landscape that looked as though a pair of giants had tired of their game of marbles, dropped their room-sized granite aggies and gone home. In front of a quaint old house with green shutters I spied a large arching rosebush that looked as if it had been growing there since the marble game had ended. It was covered in large, creamy double blooms and had the most handsome blue-green foliage imaginable. This was my introduction to *Rosa alba Maxima.*

Once called the Jacobite rose or the Great White rose, this variety was very popular in sixteenth-century Europe and was used as the emblem of the Jacobites, who supported Bonnie Prince Charlie of the House of Stuart. Alba Maxima has proven its historical longevity and, as testified by its windy home amongst the granite boulders of the Nova Scotia coast, its hardiness.

Give this summer bloomer plenty of room so that you can appreciate both the beauty and the fragrance of its blooms. In winter it will provide a colorful display of orange-red hips. This rose will root easily if taken just before flower buds open.

ALEXANDER MACKENZIE

Parentage: Queen Elizabeth × (Red Dawn × Suzanne o.p.).

Alexander Mackenzie is a well-tailored rose. Its foliage and form create an elegant backdrop for the flowers, which embroider the bush more skillfully than any threads could hope to do. The bush is upright and symmetrically arching.

Tall and tulip-like, the deep raspberry buds open to reveal a classic form with delicately folded petals curling back as the first warm days of summer draw them out. The petals gradually mellow to a deep, warm pink, and exude the fragrance of fresh-picked raspberries. On our hillside they have three successive waves of bloom during the season, the last flowers fading in September's first light frosts. After a wet period you will sometimes find the exterior petals browning, and the odd imper-fect petal may appear at the flower's base. Aside from a few stray petals, Alexander Mackenzie is a most gratifying rose to grow.

The most welcome news is that this rose is a remarkably hardy plant. It has impressive resistance to disease, although it does attract leafhoppers and sawflies. The leaves have a waxy sheen that exudes health. The deep reddish new foliage is an added extra of this extraordinary rose, complementing the dark green of the older leaves. It can be layered or propagated from softwood cuttings.

If I told you I know of a rose that is hardy, healthy, beautiful *and* fragrant, wouldn't you be tempted? Alexander Mackenzie is an important new rose.

BLANC DOUBLE DE COUBERT

Parentage: Rosa rugosa × *Sombreuil.*

This large white rose is one of the first that comes to mind when we think of fragrance. Like wines, roses have their degrees of sweetness. Blanc is definitely a sweet port, with a fragrance so strong you can actually overdose by inhaling deeply inside a freshly opening bloom.

The loosely arranged petals, clustered around the yellow center, reflect the wayward vigorous shoots of this bush, which in time, and particularly in groupings, forms an impressive hedge or informal bed. The first bloom resembles a swarm of large white butterflies resting on the deep green foliage and is a sight even for eyes jaded by the many flowers of spring. The blooms do not leave the bush till the nights get their first real chill. Although not as numerous later in the season, Blanc always has a perfumed treat for the garden wanderer.

If you are in search of a delicate, well-mannered rose, look elsewhere. Blanc is a robust grower and a thicket-type bush, sending suckers outward as it grows. This very vigor makes Blanc a valuable plant for stabilizing steep banks or creating hedges and large beds. Softwood cuttings root relatively easily if taken early in the season just before flowering, and suckers can be used.

Unless you live where winter temperatures can freeze spit before it hits the ground, you stand a chance of overwintering Blanc. This adaptable and healthy rose has been one of the most important of the truly hardy roses.

CARMENETTA

Parentage: Rosa glauca (*formerly* Rosa rubrifolia) × Rosa rugosa.

If I lived where there were only fifty frost-free days a year and where winter temperatures routinely plummet to -40° (F or C) or colder, I would be limited to growing only a few of the hardiest varieties. Carmenetta would probably be one of them.

Carmenetta is a seedling of the Red Leafed rose, a species with a lovely arching form and a reddish foliage that gives the plant a warm glow, even when not covered by its star-shaped single pink blooms. The breeder of this rose gently dusted pollen from a *rugosa* rose onto the centers of the flowers on his Red Leafed rose. He carefully saved each seed from this union, then planted and observed each as it grew. After several years one seedling in particular caught his eye most often. It was a robust arching plant with flowers that were noticeably larger than that of its siblings. Nearly ninety years later I grow this same seedling in my garden, and so can you.

The red pigments that run all through this rose also color its bark, so that the deep red new growth colorfully accents the graceful silhouette of Carmenetta in the snow. Those pigments also suffuse the veins of each flower petal, making the entire plant an enormous pink bouquet. Like first romance, Carmenetta does not last as long as we wish, but the experience is enough to make us long for our next affair. The fruit is oval, reddish purple, and Carmenetta is easy to propagate from softwood cuttings.

CHLORIS

Parentage: unknown, Rosa alba *hybrid.*

The search for the thornless rose has a long history, and even today the goal of a first-class thornless rose occupies many a breeder. Some thornless roses are available to growers. The most famous one is the Bourbon rose Zéphirine Drouhin. While hardy by most standards, this rose is not tough enough for the coldest areas. There is a rose, however, that is virtually thornless, exceptionally hardy and exceedingly beautiful. Its name is Chloris.

Chloris is a diaphanous pink that seems nearly transparent. The petals are loosely arranged around an infolded grouping of petals that form a neat button at the center. The scent of the soft, double blooms is exquisite.

This rose is easy to grow and root from softwood cuttings. It is quite vigorous, with long, deep red, erect stems that look as good after the bitter cold winter as they did when the first snow bedded them down. The foliage is of the deepest green and is a picture of health, giving the plant presence even when it's not in bloom. And on top of this, when you go collecting a fresh spray of flowers for your table, the beast will not bite.

CONSTANCE SPRY

Parentage: Belle Isis × Dainty Maid.

I received my first Constance Spry several years ago but did not know it. When my plants began to bloom I was overwhelmed by this rose's unusual, perfect form and superb color. Only it was not the variety I had ordered. Nevertheless, I told the propagators to take cuttings. Several years later I ordered Constance Spry. When it began blooming I immediately suspected that our orphan was the very same rose. Receiving the wrong rose is exasperating for any gardener, but for the nurseryman it represents a real danger, for many of these roses take two years to begin blooming. If they are not caught in time, the wrong rose can be put into the nursery beds and later sold, followed by a very embarrassing period of explanations.

If you are a peony fan, then Constance Spry will be welcome in your garden. Its beautifully formed, round, cupped flowers truly resemble the peony and are large enough to make you stop for a second look to be sure that this is a rose. The flower is a pure, bright pink with a delightful fragrance that has been likened to myrrh, and the foliage is gray-green and abundant.

In warmer climes this rose is used as a climber. Although it suffers some winterkill in our garden, making it a poor climber, it is tough enough to form a very tidy shrub. Spring pruning can make this somewhat sprawling, vigorous plant into a handsome part of the landscape. This was one "mistake" that we are glad to have in our garden.

F.J. GROOTENDORST

Parentage: Rosa rugosa × *Mme. Norbert Levavasseur.*

F.J. Grootendorst has a prolific display of small, soft red flowers, more reminiscent of carnations than roses. Its long season, hardiness and thrusting canes covered in deep green foliage have ensured it a place in the northern garden. This rose has also become an intriguing mystery to me. It has been assumed that Grootendorst was found by a Dr. De Goey from Holland in 1918. Recently, however, I read these lines from *Horticultural Horizons* by Canadian breeder Frank Leith Skinner:

"My first attempt at plant breeding was with roses. Either in 1907 or 1908, I crossed *Rosa rugosa* with one of our wild roses and this success encouraged me to try some other crosses. I used pollen of Mme. Norbert Levavasseur on *Rosa rugosa* and obtained three seedlings, one of which was identical with the variety that was to be brought out about fifteen years later as F.J. Grootendorst. It was not, however, entirely hardy, usually killing back to within a foot of the ground each winter, although it did flower quite freely on the wood that survived.

"I rather liked this rose and thinking it might do well at Ottawa I dug it up, together with some other plants and sent them on to Dr. W.T. Macoun at the Central Experimental Farm, Ottawa. The same day I also sent some plants to Professor F.W. Brodrick at the Manitoba Agricultural College. Both parcels were sent by the same railway from Roblin; no parcel reached Professor Brodrick, and the plants which he should have received were delivered to Dr. Macoun. It was too late by this time to bother about the parcel that had disappeared.

"I wrote to F.J. Grootendorst, Boskoop, Holland, after I had seen the Grootendorst rose and asked if he would care to let me know its parentage as I too was engaged in breeding roses and other plants suitable for our climate. In his reply he stated that his firm had bought the rose with the privilege of naming it, and that it was a chance seedling that had appeared among a batch of *rugosa* seedlings raised by a small grower near Boskoop. Since then I have seen it listed as having been raised in 1918 by Dr. Goey, the result of a cross between *Rosa rugosa* and Mme. Norbert Levavasseur. Mr. Herman Grootendorst told me that they had had this rose before 1914 but had been unable to market it owing to the war. There is, apparently, some doubt as to who did propagate the rose known as F.J. Grootendorst. I definitely raised an identical rose and its parentage was *Rosa rugosa* × Mme. Norbert Levavasseur."

A good story. I will let the historians find the truth. Whatever the verdict, F.J. Grootendorst will remain famous for its beauty and toughness.

Pink Grootendorst is a flesh pink sport that sometimes reverts back to the original color, as shown here.

White Grootendorst is a sport discovered by Eddie in 1962.

FRÜHLINGSGOLD

Parentage: Joanna Hill × Rosa pimpinellifolia *hybrid.*

I was once given a bundle of root pieces of the variety Harison's Yellow by a generous and dynamic lady, who was also a first-class gardener. When the plants began blooming I noticed that one was quite different. Although yellow, it was a larger and paler rose. For many years this orphan remained a mystery to me. Then one day, while reading through Beale's *Classic Roses*, I saw a picture of Frühlingsgold and immediately knew it was my mystery rose.

True to its name, Frühlingsgold ("spring gold") helps to usher in the rose season. Its large semi-double blooms are an ethereal primrose yellow. Our type of soil adds mysterious wisps of pale pink, giving the barest hint of an accent to this soft pastel flower.

The bush is a strong and resourceful plant. As this rose matures, the branches create a pattern of numerous intersecting arcs. Even these stems reflect their flower's color, the green of the new growth being suffused with goldenrod yellow until time fades them gray. The leaflets of Frühlingsgold have edges that fold under, giving the rose's foliage a soft look that becomes a quilted backdrop for the flowers.

Frühlingsgold is often budded or grafted. It can be difficult to root. Use clean, vigorous wood that is setting flower buds, the earlier in summer the better, and stick in high humidity, but do not keep wet. When roots appear, transplant as gently as possible into a good growing medium.

In the garden this rose exhibits uncommon hardiness and the tips seldom suffer from frostbite. It seems to succeed even in rather poor, dry soils, although with care and good soil, you can grow blooms whose delicate pastels will enroll you as a new member of the Frühlingsgold fan club.

GERANIUM

Parentage: Rosa moyesii *seedling.*

"Startling" might be an appropriate adjective for this plant. It would be difficult to imagine a brighter red than that possessed by this single rose. It is a shade reminiscent of Chinese red lacquer. Although blooming for only a few weeks in early summer, it deserves a space in your garden, where its long, gracefully arching stems can have their place in the sun. The triangular thorns that grow evenly spaced along the ascending shoots are quite ornamental, particularly in winter. Another endearing winter feature is the profusion of bright red hips, shaped like ancient amphorae. The leaves are small and delicate but plentiful enough to adequately clothe its bones. If you live where temperatures do not fall below −13°F (−25°C), try to locate Eddie's Jewel; it is a repeat-blooming version of this rose.

GOLDBUSCH

Parentage: *unknown*, Rosa eglanteria *hybrid.*

Although artists throughout the ages have tried to capture the essence of roses in their works, a bloom from a rose such as Goldbusch relegates all these attempts to the class of pale imitations. We paid very little for our Goldbusch, but this work of art is now among our garden's most cherished possessions.

Goldbusch was bred from the Eglantine or Sweet Briar rose, and its long arching canes reflect its heritage and make it a good candidate for a climber. Like the Sweet Briar, its foliage is sweetly scented. Even more impressive to me is the healthy glow of the medium green leaves. Little if any blackspot or mildew mar the backdrop they provide for the exquisite blooms. This lovely rose is also easy to root from softwood cuttings.

The tight pyramidal buds are a deep honey color with just a hint of orange. They open into a semi-double flower of alluring bright yellow. The fragrance is a fitting asset of this wonderful flower.

It is difficult to find any faults with this captivating rose. It seems quite hardy, although I doubt it will survive in the very coldest sites.

HANSA

Parentage: Rosa rugosa *hybrid.*

Venerable bushes of Hansa grow on innumerable old farmsites throughout the countryside where I live. In the suburbs, younger plants have appeared, taken there by the sons and daughters of those who first planted these roses. For many, this variety represents the term "hardy rose." These long-lived plants form immense mounds, often hollow on the inside from lack of light. Throughout the early summer, they bloom with large mauve-red flowers. It is generally very healthy with no serious insect problems. Its beauty, tenacity, hardiness and ease of propagation have made Hansa common, the highest compliment in horticulture.

One of the most enduring appeals of Hansa is the heady draught of fragrance on a still summer evening. Although you can eat the petals, those after more substance will delight in chewing around the core of a Hansa rose hip. This rose produces a profusion of deep orange-red fruits that are large and meaty, just right for the makers of rosehip tea, those who cherish late autumn color, or the birds.

HARISON'S YELLOW

Parentage: Rosa pimpinellifolia × Rosa foetida persiana.

Of all the colors in roses, yellow is the color that northern growers desire the most, perhaps because it is the most difficult color to obtain in a hardy rose. This fact makes Harison's Yellow a special rose, for it is both deep yellow and incredibly hardy.

Strangely enough, this winter-hardy rose was developed in Texas, quite far from the numbing cold of the north. An amateur rose fancier named Harison crossed the Scotch Briar rose with the Persian Yellow, another hardy yellow rose, and Harison's Yellow was the result. Most people consider this variety the original "yellow rose of Texas," made famous by the well-known song of the same name. Whether in the scorching heat of a Texas summer or in the deep freeze of a northern winter, this adaptable rose has earned a place in the hearts of many.

Harison's Yellow is an early bloomer like its parents. The numerous small buds turn themselves inside out to reveal the sulfur yellow petals hidden within. The delicate branches of this unassuming shrub suddenly become arching sprays of sunshine. This tropical display lasts but a few weeks and we are left with a rather coarse and humble bush for the remainder of the season, but, like the sun, Harison's Yellow can't shine forever, and if it did, we would not appreciate its radiance.

To propagate, take cuttings early in the season from wood just setting flower buds. Keep in high humidity, but not overly wet. When roots appear, carefully transplant into a good growing medium and carefully harden them off to drier conditions. It is most often budded or grafted. Suckers can be used.

JOHN DAVIS

Parentage: Rosa kordesii × (*Red Dawn* × *Suzanne o.p.*).

Occasionally a rose appears that causes an instant buzz in the nursery world. John Davis cuttings were sent to our nursery several years ago and were planted in the display garden. They began blooming even as tiny plants, and by the third year we had people begging for just one plant. Try as I might, I simply could not get this rose from any of the usual sources. They were like us, trying desperately to create as many stock plants as they could. New as it is, John Davis has the makings of a star.

When they unfold, the semi-double blooms of John Davis flatten their outside petals, leaving an attractive tulip-shaped center of the remaining folded petals. They are a deep orchid-pink at this stage. Gradually the cen-ter unfolds until the blossom lies open, fading to a lighter shade of pink as it does so. Once in bloom this rose always has flowers, being close to everblooming.

The bush is vigorous but somewhat sprawling, eventually becoming a large, lax shrub. This rose could probably be successfully trained into a medium-sized climber. It is also one of our hardiest new varieties. Our specimens have never winterkilled in the slightest, and I have no doubt that it will prove hardy into the far north. As with so many of the Explorer Series roses, it is also highly disease resistant, although it attracts leafhoppers and sawflies early in the season. It can be propagated from softwood cuttings.

MARIE VICTORAN

Parentage: Arthur Bell × L83 (Rosa kordesii × G49).

It fascinates me that the colors we see in a rose are those that have not been absorbed by the petals, the reflected parts of the light spectrum—the discards, as it were. Each rose reflects a unique blend of colors. One of the most unusual new reflections occurs off the blossoms of Marie Victoran. The petals of this Canadian Explorer rose bounce back silvery pink, with edges and undersides of soft yellow. The combination is enchanting. The scent released by this flower is a perfect balance between sweetness and lightness, its draw a most wonderful addiction. This is also an exquisitely structured flower. The buds are pointed somewhat like a hybrid tea rose and unfurl into a symmetrical double bloom. The bush is moderately vigorous and hardy enough to grow well in Zone 4, with only slight winterkill. Disease does not plague this rose, although some blackspot will appear on the older foliage. This is a rose to cherish.

MRS. ANTHONY WATERER

Parentage: Rosa rugosa × General Jacqueminot.

It confounds me why this rose is not more popular. It has so many good features and yet remains one of the lesser known *rugosa* roses. If my words of praise encourage you to obtain this rugged and reliable variety, I will consider my efforts worthwhile.

Mrs. Anthony Waterer is an excellent grower. Its vigorous shoots reach upward and gradually arch outward to form a handsome large bush. It is a good specimen on its own or will create a tall and colorful hedge if combined with others. The healthy foliage is seldom damaged by disease and forms a green foil worthy of its blossoms.

The flowers are unusual for a *rugosa* as they are well shaped and a deep and true crimson from center to edge. As the bud unfolds, the outer petals form a circle that delightfully frames the cupped center. Emanating from these bright flowers is as lovely a fragrance as one could wish. Best of all, these richly hued blossoms are produced abundantly throughout the entire season. This rose roots well from softwood cuttings taken early in the season just before flowering.

Mrs. Anthony Waterer was introduced at the end of the last century. Discriminating growers have ensured its survival for nearly one hundred years. Perhaps at last more gardeners will be able to understand what these few growers have always known and give Mrs. Anthony Waterer her long overdue recognition.

MME. PLANTIER

Parentage: unknown, Rosa alba *hybrid.*

As I gaze out my window through the crystals of snow settling on the leafless stems of the rose bushes, my eyes are drawn to a fountain of arching grass-green stems. These stems belong to one of the most famous of the *Rosa alba* hybrids, Mme. Plantier. This robust grower will survive our frigid winters, and next summer those same green stems will be weighed down with hundreds of pure white quartered blooms whose ethereal vapors spur the rose grower to keep forking on the manure.

Give this plant plenty of room. In warmer climes the long stems can be used to cover walls or trellises. In very cold areas the tips will kill back some, but this rose loves to grow. It is not a suckering plant, however, so it will stay somewhat contained horizontally. We never concern ourselves with disease affecting Mme. Plantier. Any spots that may occur on the lustrous, deep green foliage are so few that they are of no consequence. It is as easy to root as any rose I know.

QUADRA

Parentage: B08 (A15 (Queen Elizabeth × Arthur Bell) × D35 (Simonet double red × Von Scharnhorst)) × L25 (Rosa kordesii × D07 (Red Dawn × Suzanne)).

I like to think of plants and animals as fragile crystals growing out of the minerals on the earth's surface into the gases of the atmosphere. Quadra is a rose crystal of exceptional rarity. Hundreds of intense red petals are arranged in a symmetrical pattern reminiscent of the older *gallica* roses, once so common in European gardens. The petals curve, peony-like, toward the center as the rose opens. When the flower expands, these same petals recurve outward, creating a rounded cushion with the texture of soft quilted velvet. While the fragrance is not strong, the bouquet is reminiscent of fresh fruit.

The bush that supports this extravagant arrangement of petals is one of great beauty as well. The new foliage is tinted red. The surface of the older leaves looks freshly polished, and a subtle hint of red remains locked within the veins. The bush is vigorous and healthy and will endure temperatures that would wither red roses of comparable color and form. Quadra forms an upright and somewhat arched shrub that should prove useful as a low climber. It is easy to propagate. This crystal is deserving of your most special setting.

ROSERAIE DE L'HAY

Parentage: unknown, Rosa rugosa hybrid.

Early every summer morning it is my job to pick two or three roses from each variety growing in the nursery. They are arranged in bowls in large concentric circles so that you can compare the blossoms on the table with ease. This daily exercise is like a mantra. I chart the same course each day and visit the roses in the same order, searching the bushes for the most perfect opening blooms. It is both calming and exhilarating. The last bush I visit is Roseraie de L'Hay. It reaches well over my head, with dark green foliage and large double blooms that

entice the nose with heavy, sweet perfume.

The dictionary describes the color magenta as deep purplish red. Roseraie de L'Hay is perfect magenta. There are newer *Rosa rugosa* hybrids that may have a bit more late-season bloom, but few can match the effect of this rose's fascinating petal arrangement. When the high-centered buds open, the outer petals lay flat, the middle petals twist like crepe and the innermost petals remain somewhat higher. This easy-to-root rose is absolutely hardy and never shows any sign of disease.

ROBUSTA

Parentage: Rosa rugosa × *seedling.*

Fallen petals of a Robusta rose have become a meal for a scavenging beetle. Above, new crimson flowers unfold. Not all roses have this ability to repeatedly generate new flowers. Many, having performed their yearly fertility rite, pass into the summer's heat clothed only in their greenery. Robusta belongs to that elite and much prized group of roses that are remontant, or repeat-blooming.

Although Robusta is simply formed, the size and crimson color ensure that this rose will take a backseat to no others. It is indeed a robust rose, and easy to root from softwood cuttings. Viciously thorned stems thrust upward from the plant's base to form a tall, vertical shrub, well suited to frame smaller plants. The combination of large, textured dark green foliage and wine-red stems is visually exciting as well. A delicate, fruity fragrance emanates from Robusta, so those who garden for their nose as well as their eyes will not be disappointed.

A 50% winter killback is average with this rose in our garden, but it inevitably makes a spirited comeback, and by mid-July we are tipping our hats to the skilled hands of Wilhelm Kordes for giving us another healthy and incredibly lovely rose.

SARAH VAN FLEET

Parentage: Rosa rugosa × *My Maryland.*

Many people have told me that they don't bother growing shrub roses because the plants don't bloom long enough. This attitude is, sadly, a widely held one, mainly because many of the better varieties are not available to the public. Many of these roses are new in the nursery trade, and it takes many years to get enough out in the landscape to create a demand. Until recently there has been little incentive for the nursery trade to propagate shrub roses. The public seemed uninterested in the shrubs. New trends in gardening, however, have dramatically changed the situation.

Varieties like Sarah Van Fleet will go a long way toward revising people's perception of shrub roses. This plant gives a perpetual show of fragrant, clear pink, semi-double blooms. While not quite as hardy as some of its *rugosa* relatives, Sarah Van Fleet does very well in our garden even in the worst years, killing back only the top half of its vigorous, upright shoots. In warmer areas this rose will form a tall shrub. Under more northern conditions it will stay somewhat smaller, but each year's shoots are remarkably tall. It does suffer from a bit of blackspot on the lower leaves, and I have seen a touch of mildew in damp conditions. I have read that this variety is inclined to rust, although I have not seen any on our plants. Although this makes the plant sound like a mass of disease, we have found it generally quite healthy and easy to root from softwood cuttings.

SCABROSA

Parentage: A selected Rosa rugosa *seedling.*

Although cursed with a most unfortunate name, this wonderful rose is a delight in the garden. Its immense cerise single blooms are its major claim to fame, but I think its most important feature is the bush. Given proper space, this rose will fill a sizable area. It is vigorous and dense with lush, deep green foliage, making it an excellent background plant or a luxuriant hedge. The prolific flowers continue throughout the entire season, making the bush a colorful as well as prominent part of the landscape. In fall, this bush becomes a beacon of yellow, red and golden hues. Large, orange-red hips are sprinkled liberally throughout this iridescent foliage, making Scabrosa one of the most attractive roses at the season's end.

This rose becomes more impressive as it ages. When young, Scabrosa is simply another pretty *rugosa* rose. When older, it commands attention with its impressive stature and floral abundance. It is certainly one of the hardiest roses you can grow, and you never need worry about dragging out the sprayer, as it is virtually immune to disease. It roots well from softwood cuttings taken early in the season, and suckers can be used. Scabrosa is tough, dependable, floriferous and beautiful. It is hard to ask more of a rose.

SCHARLACHGLUT

Parentage: Poinsettia × *Alika (Rosa gallica grandiflora).*

Scharlachglut comes close to the look of crimson crushed velvet. And if ever there were a rose to turn the heads of those who say "I'm not interested in single roses," this is the one. The English translation of "Scharlachglut" is "Scarlet glow" or "Scarlet fire." Neither name can quite capture the intensity of this rose's color.

Part of Scharlachglut's effect lies in its size. It has the largest blossoms in our garden, and, in keeping with this grand design, the bush is also large, with thrusting canes that droop slightly. Although a bit open, the bush forms an adequate background for its flowers. Judicious pruning will help to thicken the bush and improve the overall presence of this rose.

We had few hopes for Scharlachglut when it was first planted, but although it requires some pruning of dead wood each spring, this rose has proved tough. It is generally very healthy, and can be rooted from softwood cuttings. After four years it now commands a prominent place at our garden's entrance, having convinced us that it intends to stay.

THÉRÈSE BUGNET

Parentage: (Rosa acicularis × Rosa kamtchatica) × (Rosa amblyotis × Rosa rugosa plena) × *Betty Bland*.

There are many unsung plant propagators in farflung places who never receive the acclamation they deserve. Georges Bugnet of Legal, Alberta, is such a person. Emigrating from his native France in 1905, Bugnet arrived in a land with rich soil but intensely cold winters. Roses had to withstand temperatures that regularly fell to -40° (F or C) or colder. Using the native roses, as well as roses he imported from such exotic places as the Kamchatka Peninsula in the Soviet Union, Bugnet created some of the hardiest garden roses in existence. One in particular is a rose of uncommon distinction – Thérèse Bugnet.

Thérèse Bugnet is a remarkable rose, not only for its unusual hardiness but for the large and intensely fragrant blossoms that occur so prolifically from late spring to late summer. When this impressive, fountain-like bush first blooms, the foliage is barely visible. Later flushes are less showy, but Thérèse Bugnet is rarely out of bloom during the season. The tissue-paper texture of this soft pink rose has an informal look, yet the plant has lost the wild look of its parents and is sophisticated enough for virtually any garden.

Thérèse Bugnet also gives color to the landscape in winter. The well-balanced silhouette of this vigorous bush is a deep clear red. These same stems have the added advantage of being almost thornless near the flowers, making them much easier to pick for bouquets than many of the shrub roses. This rose is extremely easy to root from softwood cuttings.

WILLIAM LOBB

Parentage: *unknown*, Rosa centifolia muscosa *hybrid*.

People are slowly awakening to the immense body of plants that has been neglected and that deserves a more important place in the garden. Perhaps with this exciting trend gaining momentum, we will soon see such varieties as William Lobb in more gardens.

William Lobb is the English name of a French rose, Duchesse d'Istrie. To complicate matters, its sensuous purple-crimson blooms inspired the name Old Velvet Moss. Whatever name you prefer, this rose is a welcome addition to the northern garden. Its extreme vigor is matched by its tremendous hardiness. In our garden the long, thorny stems are rarely touched by even the coldest winters, and after a few years of extraordinary growth, the bush becomes an imposing part of any rose bed. For this reason, be sure to give the plant room. As well, you may want to give it some support, as its long stems are somewhat lax and the numerous blossoms, which come in large clusters, weigh the stems down.

This is one of the Moss roses. The interesting soft bristles that cover the buds and upper stems of these roses are quite abundant in William Lobb. The flower itself is very double and well formed with a delightful fragrance. Although only medium in size, the sheer numbers of blooms will create a dazzling display. William Lobb is also fairly easy to root from softwood cuttings.

**Schneezwerg's powerful fragrance
and hardiness are exceptional.**

8

Semi-vigorous Shrubs

Shrubs growing up to 6 ft. (1.8 m)

AGNES
ALAIN BLANCHARD
CARDINAL RICHELIEU
CELESTIAL
CHARLES DE MILLS
DART'S DASH
DR. MERKELEY
FÉLICITÉ PARMENTIER
GEORGE VANCOUVER
HENRI MARTIN
HUNTER
J.P. CONNELL
KAKWA
KARL FÖRSTER
KÖNIGIN VON DÄNEMARK
LINDA CAMPBELL
MAIDEN'S BLUSH
MARIE BUGNET
MINETTE
MORDEN CENTENNIAL
PERSIAN YELLOW
PIERETTE PAVEMENT
POLAREIS
PURPLE PAVEMENT
RAUBRITTER
ROSA MUNDI
SCHNEEZWERG
SNOW PAVEMENT
SUAVEOLENS

AGNES

Parentage: Rosa rugosa × Rosa foetida persiana.

The *rugosa* rose is, without a doubt, the species most utilized by northern growers. Not only are many *rugosas* important garden varieties, but this species has been extensively hybridized to produce some of our most exciting hardy roses. A great deal of work has been done to produce hardy yellow *rugosa* hybrids. Agnes is one of the few successes of these endeavors.

This rose has many attributes that recommend it as deserving a favored place in your garden. The delightful fruity fragrance of this rose is as essential a part of its character as its pastel petals, which subtly shift from apricot to light yellow to ivory. These flowers adorn a bush that is exceptionally hardy, and the crinkled lime green leaves are seldom if ever bothered by disease. Agnes is usually budded or grafted. Suckers can be used. Cuttings should be taken just before flowering early in the season. Avoid overmisting. A humidity tent works well.

Some may find this rose too fragile. Its petals are delicate and will not stand up to heavy wind and rain. This lack of substance can be called a fault, but the loose, carefree blooms of Agnes have an undeniable charm that stiff, more formal flowers can never achieve, a crown for fairies rather than kings.

ALAIN BLANCHARD

Parentage: Rosa centifolia × Rosa gallica *hybrid.*

There are a great number of *Rosa gallica* hybrids that deserve a place in the northern garden, and it is difficult to choose those that stand out as exceptional because so many are fascinating. Some have immense blooms, others an inordinate number of petals. Alain Blanchard is neither a giant nor very double; what it has is unique coloration. The red petals are spotted with darker red patches. Instead of looking sickly or weird, the combination is both appealing and fascinating. It would be interesting to know if this coloring was on the original plant or if its genes have mutated. Like most *gallicas*, the blossoms are quite fragrant. Alain Blanchard is also a hardy bush that is easy to grow and does not get overly large. The leaves are deepest green and heavily textured. It roots fairly well. A special rose for the collector.

CARDINAL RICHELIEU

Parentage: unknown, Rosa gallica *hybrid.*

If you are a purple person, this elderly representative of the *Rosa gallica* tribe is for you. Its mum-like very double bloom is the quintessential purple amongst hardy roses. The perfectly symmetrical flowers appear in profusion in early summer on a dense plant that usually grows no higher than 3 ft. (1 m). Our bushes bloom for four to five weeks. The last flowers on our plants exhibit a curious trait. Through the center of each flower a small stalk with a stunted version of another flower emerges. This process is called proliferation, and although not unique to Cardinal Richelieu, this variety produces these aberrations with a regularity I have never seen elsewhere.

This is one of the toughest *gallicas,* hardy to at least –30°C (–35°F). Its leaves may show slight blackspot near the bottom of the bush, but this is never enough to mar the appearance of the plant. Cuttings taken early in the season root well.

CELESTIAL

Parentage: unknown, Rosa alba *hybrid.*

Never judge a plant by its name. When you are in the business of selling plants, you realize how much people react to the emotional connotations of names. Give a dog of a plant a catchy name and it will sell . . . for a while. Ultimately, however, a plant's merits become its best advertisement and determine its staying power.

Celestial is a nurseryman's dream come true. For here is a name that conjures up images of heavenly choirs or colorful galaxies floating in space and the flower actually lives up to these visions of ethereal beauty. For this is a rose of the purest pink and the most delicate of textures. This fine and very old double form of the *Rosa alba* has remained popular for centuries.

These (dare I use the word) heavenly smelling roses are set on a very neat bush with bluish-green foliage. Though perhaps not for subarctic areas, most northern gardeners should have no trouble overwintering this carefree and rewarding rose, or propagating it from softwood cuttings.

CHARLES DE MILLS

Parentage: unknown, Rosa gallica *hybrid.*

On a warm July day I noticed a slightly exasperated-looking elderly woman working her way purposefully through the garden. As I approached her to ask if I could help, she looked up and fairly shouted at me, "Don't you have any double roses here?" I pointed out several roses near her that were double. "Oh, not that kind. I mean *really* double." I realized that this lady was looking not for a double rose but for what is called a quartered rose, one with so many petals that, lacking room, the flower seems to fold itself into four equal parts. I led her to the Charles de Mills, and when she saw the large and extravagant blooms, an instant calm spread across her face. "Now *that's* a rose," she lectured me.

Charles de Mills's flowers are a glowing blend of rich red and purple with the edges shading toward the deepest of pinks. Unlike many of the shrub roses, Charles de Mills maintains an elegant cupped form even when fully open, and a bush covered with these large, vibrant flowers forms an elegant centerpiece in any garden. Add to this the flower's intense perfume and it is not surprising that this is one of the most popular of the *Rosa gallicas.*

The deep green foliage is rarely bothered by disease, although the occasional blackspot will show up on older leaves or where air circulation is poor. The bush forms a symmetrical globe with slightly lax stems that are fairly free from thorns. Although it's not for the very coldest of sites, most gardeners should be able to grow this rose, for it is quite hardy. It is also reasonably easy to root from softwood cuttings.

DART'S DASH

Parentage: unknown, Rosa rugosa *hybrid.*

This *rugosa* rose is a scaled-down version of the well-known Hansa rose. Its flowers are the same mauvered color and have the same general petal formation and similar growth habits and foliage, but Dart's Dash flowers for a much longer period and the bush is more compact. A long flowering season is an advantage for any rose, but in modern horticulture small has become beautiful, as people try to fit plants into small-scale urban and suburban sites, and Dart's Dash, with its smaller stature, can be a useful component of such gardens.

This rose's large orange globular hips have enough flesh that the delicate nibbler, chewing around the seed core, can have an enjoyable snack. One of my favorite treats is eating Dart's Dash hips just after the first light frosts have softened them. This culinary pleasure is particularly enjoyable because, at the same time, I can inhale the strong fragrance of the blossoms, which even that late in the season are still gracing this most interesting rose. To propagate Dart's Dash, take softwood cuttings from wood early in the season.

DR. MERKELEY
Parentage: unknown.

At the end of World War I, a Canadian soldier arrived home from his duty in Siberia with a most unusual souvenir. It was a very double pink rose with a heavenly scent, only this rose came with roots attached. The rose was eventually brought to the attention of the Canadian breeder Frank L. Skinner of Dropmore, Manitoba. He immediately saw the value of this ultra-hardy rose and began growing it. He introduced it to the world in 1924 as Dr. Merkeley, to commemorate the man who had first grown it in North America.

This rose has largely been maintained by collectors, and has been difficult to obtain. The explosion of interest in shrub roses has resulted in this obscure rose resurfacing to grace the gardens of northern growers. It is a dense shrub, wider than high, with extraordinarily healthy foliage. It flowers quite late in the season and continues until early fall with its deep pink blooms.

FÉLICITÉ PARMENTIER
Parentage: unknown, Rosa alba *hybrid.*

People judge scent in much the same way as taste, and what smells sublime to one person will be objectionable to another. However, I have yet to meet anyone who turns up his nose at Félicité Parmentier. This old *Rosa alba* hybrid might be considered the Holy Grail for pilgrims of perfume. The fragrant blooms are tight clusters of blush pink petals, artfully arranged into symmetrical bowls. The bush is a well-mannered and somewhat low-growing shrub with deep green textured leaves that are not overly troubled by disease. If cuttings are taken early, they root well. Félicité Parmentier does not repeat, but you can expect many weeks of enjoyment from this quintessential *alba* rose.

GEORGE VANCOUVER

Parentage: L83 (Rosa kordesii × G49) × seedling of complex origin.

The Canadian Explorer Series of roses has given the northern rose grower some of the most reliable varieties now available. One of the later selections is George Vancouver. This superb introduction is one of the hardiest of the non-*rugosa* types. Plants that have endured −30°F (−35°C) show little or no damage. It is also a plant with a neat habit and deep green, shiny foliage. It is not overly vigorous, instead forming a wide rounded bush with colorful, deep red stems.

The flowers start in early summer and in fall are still laden with bloom. Blossoms are borne in clusters. Each semi-double bloom is a neat arrangement of scalloped petals, symmetrical but not stiff. The color of the flowers is a subtle blend of red and orange as the buds open, giving a subdued scarlet look, fading to dark pink before falling cleanly off the bush. This is a rose that will win your admiration and affection over the years. It is a very easy rose to root.

HENRI MARTIN

Parentage: Rosa × centifolia muscosa.

The Moss roses are a most unusual group. They had their beginnings in the seventeenth century, when one of the Cabbage roses underwent a strange mutation. Some of its branches grew odd glandular structures on the flower stems and calyxes that have a remarkable resemblance to moss. This freak rose was cultivated and eventually bred to create new Moss roses with a wide range of flower colors. Although a number of these cultivars are quite hardy and well adapted to northern gardens, Henri Martin has a special place in my garden because of its masses of crimson flowers.

In late spring Henri Martin is a fountain of blossom. Each cluster is carried by rather slender, wiry stems with thorns that are deceptively harmless-looking. The bush is generally upright but somewhat lax and spreading. Even though we need to prune Henri reasonably hard each spring to remove winterkilled stem ends, most of the bush survives, and its ability to spring back is remarkable. The deep orange hips are small and vase-shaped, and Henri Martin is reasonably easy to root.

Moss roses add a distinctive and curious bit of variety to the palette of common roses, and isn't variety the spice that drives most of us to seek yet more plants to fill our overflowing garden beds?

HUNTER

Parentage: Rosa rugosa rubra × *Independence.*

True red is a rare color in the *rugosa* roses, which are usually a reddish purple or mauve. This relative newcomer to the group is a spectacular crimson. Its velvety petals are gently and symmetrically folded into a very alluring fully double form.

The color alone would make this rose interesting, but what makes it important is the intense, dark green, shiny foliage that forms a perfect background for the flowers, its neat and compact growth habit and the fact that this rose is a continuous bloomer.

It is difficult to find any faults with this wonderful rose. The only disappointment for me is that it is not as ironclad as many of the *rugosas*. In our area this rose will kill back slightly, but it bounces back each spring, and we will gladly put up with a little extra pruning to have Hunter grace our garden all summer. To propagate cuttings can be taken early in the season just before flowering.

J.P. CONNELL

Parentage: Arthur Bell × open pollinated seedling of Von Scharnhorst.

For those who look, the rose world has clues that can help to identify the different varieties. Examine the pattern of thorns on a stem of J.P. Connell. You will see a random pattern of short needles, a pattern different from every other rose, much like our fingerprints are unique to each of us. I have already imprinted this rose's thorn pattern in my mind, for I intend to grow this new Canadian rose.

Although prey to blackspot, the disease that haunts nearly all yellow roses, J.P. Connell fills an important niche in the inventory of hardy roses. Wave after wave of symmetrical, fully double and high-centered blooms appear all season. The first year's flowers may appear washed-out; however, as the plant establishes itself, the blossoms become larger, more profuse and colored a rich, creamy yellow. The plant is upright with plentiful rich green foliage and stiff yellow-green stems that hold up their elegant blooms.

With a little extra attention, this valuable introduction can transform a piece of your garden into an exciting showcase for one of the best new hardy yellow roses. Layering may be the best way to propagate J.P. Connell, which is moderately difficult to root.

KAKWA

Parentage: unknown, Rosa pimpinellifolia *hybrid.*

As the late spring nights lose that cool edge and the early spring flowers are reduced to simple greenery, the rose grower's anticipation heightens. The sight of those first unfolding buds is exhilarating and rejuvenating. In our garden it is the Kakwa that first appears. Almost overnight, this reliable and carefree rose becomes blanketed so thickly with blossoms that the foliage is virtually hidden under their delicate weight. This petaled coverlet is creamy white from a distance, but as you approach, the subtle pink tones of these double blooms become apparent. Another wonderful aspect of this early rose is its intense fragrance. I recommend you keep your nose at a slight distance from the flowers. Putting your nose into a Kakwa blossom is a bit like sticking it into a bottle of perfume – overpowering.

The bush is an extremely adaptable one. It will grow even in fairly poor soils and even prefers a lighter, well-drained soil. Although not a large plant, Kakwa will slowly mound upward to form a compact and dense shrub. It is a remarkably tough and hardy plant, easy to root, and will grow for most any northern gardener.

Although few roses have such an effect in bloom, Kakwa soon gives way to the many roses vying for our attentions. It is as if it gives everything it has in one exuberant burst of energy and then collapses to await the raising of the next spring curtain. Some may call it a bit part, but it acts its role with such energy that I would hate to think of the play without it.

KARL FÖRSTER

Parentage: Frau Karl Drushki × Rosa pimpinellifolia altaica.

Some roses have a way of tapping you on the shoulder and saying, "Take a look at me." My first Karl Förster plants sat at the edge of the garden for two years without attracting much attention. Then, in their third spring, they erupted with a display that took us by surprise. Shapely pointed buds by the hundreds unfolded into loose blossoms the color of whipped cream, until the foliage virtually disappeared under this unique petaled topping.

Karl Förster would not let us forget this extravaganza. As a reminder, it continued to bloom throughout the summer and early fall, an amazing feat for a Scotch rose. An added feature of this prolific bloomer is the red color of the new stems. Contrasted against the gray-green leaves, they lend a characteristic look to this relatively new rose.

All these wonderful attributes mean nothing to us if the rose does not perform well in our merciless winters. Karl Förster has passed the test with exceptional honors. It seems to have inherited the toughness of its Scotch rose parent as well as the flowering ability of its hybrid tea parent – a near perfect combination. Karl Förster is often budded or grafted. It can be rooted from softwood cuttings, but requires careful attention just after rooting or it can drop its leaves and die.

KÖNIGIN VON DÄNEMARK

Parentage: unknown, Rosa alba *hybrid.*

The Queen of Denmark is definitely a member of the royal family of older shrub roses. Many rose fanciers have a special place in their hearts and in their gardens for this most attractive and reliable rose. Although not as large as many other shrub roses, its classic flowers are artfully arranged into a well-formed cup shape that contains so many petals they seem to swirl around the button center. The pure pink tone of this rose is deeper than many of the *Rosa alba* group, fading gently to soft pink before the petals drop. The fragrance that emanates from the Queen befits nobility and is one more reason for the continuing popularity of this old rose, which is reasonably easy to root.

Generally, it is a pleasure to prune the *alba* roses because they are not as thorny as most shrub roses, but be sure to put on your gloves for this rose. Its stems, although not as vicious as those of the *rugosa* roses, make you pay for the dismemberment that you inflict on them. The bush is a nicely shaped tall mound clothed in handsome gray-green foliage. Like all *albas*, Königin von Dänemark flowers but once. However, the flowers that crown this distinguished rose are the highlights of a most glorious reign. Long live the Queen.

LINDA CAMPBELL

Parentage: Anytime × Rugosa Magnifica.

Ralph Moore is one of the most dynamic rose breeders the world has known. He has created fascinating color combinations, oak-shaped leaves and many other wonders. His use of *Rosa rugosa* for some of his crosses has given the hardy rose grower this gem. The bush arches upward and outward. The stems have a texture faintly reminiscent of velvety new deer antlers, only in red and green. There is no hesitation in coming up with a definition of petal color for this rose: it is red, red, red. The double flowers are borne on clusters so large that a single stem in hand is a bouquet. Keep this plant well fed and happy and it will create a red, red, red temple of color.

Temperatures colder than –22°F (–30°C) will cause some winter damage to stem tips, but even when pruned back by Arctic highs, they rebound. Resistance to blackspot is fair, but lower leaves will be affected when conditions favor this disease. Mildews and rusts are not problems. This is an easy rose to root.

MAIDEN'S BLUSH

Parentage: unknown, Rosa alba *hybrid.*

There are actually two forms of this popular rose. The most common form is Maiden's Blush Great. The less common is Maiden's Blush Small. The only real difference between the two is the comparative size of the bush and flower. Whichever form, it is difficult to find a rose that creates more response from people than Maiden's Blush. That this rose is still popular after 500 years is a testament to its immense appeal. I can think of no other rose with such an intoxicating aroma, such sensuous color or such perfection of form.

The bush is a moderate size with stiffly erect stems and blue-tinted foliage that shows a bit of blackspot but is otherwise healthy and abundant. Like so many of its *Rosa alba* kin, Maiden's Blush is very hardy. In late spring heavenly scented blossoms of warmest blush pink arrive in great numbers. A good deal of this rose's charm is due to the informally arranged and gently folded petals which, although neatly contained, have an endearing character that must be seen to be understood. When the Maiden's Blush comes into bloom, the rose season becomes complete for us.

This rose, aptly and more sensuously named Cuisse de Nymph (nymph's thighs) in France, will continue to be one of the most popular of the older shrub roses. For me the only disappointment is that it never lasts long enough. Maiden's Blush is generally budded or grafted. It is fairly easy to root, but blackspot can pose a problem under greenhouse conditions, causing the leaves to drop about the time the roots form.

MARIE BUGNET

Parentage: (Thérèse Bugnet × unnamed seedling) × F.J. Grootendorst.

This rose is slowly rising from obscurity to claim its overdue recognition. Its sister plant, Thérèse Bugnet, is known throughout the rose world, but Marie remained unknown except to a few collectors of heritage roses. It is not a tall plant but does spread rapidly by suckering, making it unwelcome in the tidy bed but a perfect rose for a bank or low hedge. Its *Rosa rugosa* heritage is clearly visible in its textured leaves, which rarely show any disease. The double blooms are purest white and very shapely, and they continue to appear till frost. If there is a fault in this rose it is the delicate substance of the petals. In wet weather the outer petals can become saturated and brown, not allowing the bud to open fully. However, this fault should not discourage the northern gardener from planting Marie, for though its flowers are delicate, the bush is tenacious and will survive temperatures of −40° (F or C) with ease. It roots fairly easily.

MINETTE

Parentage: unknown, probably Rosa alba *hybrid.*

Many people bring in rose cuttings for identification or propagation that have been in their families for decades or longer. It was in this way that I was introduced to this tough, long-lived rose. Once I started looking, I found it everywhere. Even my next-door neighbors had a small hedge growing in front of their farmhouse. An elderly lady with a small patch in front of her house told me how her father had ripped them all out because they were "getting everywhere," but several had reappeared and she still lovingly tended them decades after her father had died. This is indeed a survivor. Its vigor and health ensured that it weathered the winters as well as the abuse and neglect of those who may have inherited it.

Those who love to garden grow Minette for its attractive double form, sweet perfume and delicate blush pink petals. The bush is very disease-resistant and grows to around 4 ft. (1.2 m). The leaf edges curl slightly downward, giving the foliage a soft quilted look. It is easy to root. The only strike against this tough rose is a tendency to brown in wet weather. When conditions are right, however, this rose is exquisite. In Sweden it has proven so hardy that it is as common as in my neighborhood and has acquired a Swedish name, Suionum.

Recently, this rose's heritage has been questioned by several knowledgeable rosarians who think that its true name may be "Banshee," not "Minette." The origins of "Banshee" remain a mystery, as it seems to have appeared in the mid-18th century in both Europe and North America. It has been suggested that rather than a **R. alba** hybrid, this may be a hybrid between **R. damascena** and **R. virginiana**. We wish the horticultural sleuths well in their quest for truth.

MORDEN CENTENNIAL

Parentage: Prairie Princess × (White Bouquet × (J.W. Fargo × Assiniboine)).

This 1980 Canadian selection is a treasure. The bush is very vigorous and upright-growing, with healthy deep green foliage. In my garden it only suffers winter injury when temperatures fall below −22°F (−30°C). Even when the tops are killed back, the base rebounds and produces pink double blooms of near perfect symmetry. The large flowers are arranged in clusters that make ideal centerpieces for your table. Morden Centennial has a pleasant, albeit light, perfume. It roots relatively well from cuttings.

PERSIAN YELLOW

Parentage: Rosa foetida persiana.

Virtually every yellow rose can trace its color back to this double form of *Rosa foetida*. Originally found in southwestern Asia, *Rosa foetida* is shrouded in the mists of ancient history. Around 1837 this double form appeared and was soon introduced into European and North American gardens. Rose breeders continue to use it for its rich, golden color and double form. As well as transmitting its color, Persian Yellow has contributed its susceptibility to blackspot to the genetic "soup" of modern roses. But it's hard to complain about some spots when the alternative is a world without yellow roses.

The flowers of Persian Yellow appear in late spring and continue for three or four weeks. The form is globular. The fragrance is light and unusual, although definitely not fetid, as its Latin name would suggest.

This very hardy bush is generally upright with a tendency to sprawl as it ages. Its branches are somewhat thin and appear a bit wayward. It is not totally ungainly, and as it matures, this rose assumes a fairly full and impressive stature. This is definitely one rose to prune with restraint. Its flowers arise from the old wood, so drastic spring pruning will severely limit your blooms. As well, this rose does not seem to respond well to heavy pruning, and continued aggressive pruning may kill the plant.

Persian Yellow is one of the few varieties that I treat with wettable sulfur. If not treated, it will drop most of its leaves shortly after flowering. If you live in areas with humid summers, blackspot will be a problem you must deal with. Those in drier areas will find Persian Yellow fairly easy to grow, particularly as it is more tolerant of poor, sandy soils than most roses. The rose is very difficult to root from softwood cuttings. Use new wood and avoid overmisting. It is most often budded or grafted.

PIERETTE PAVEMENT

Parentage: unknown, Rosa rugosa *hybrid.*

The European roses, grouped together for marketing purposes in North America as the Pavement roses, are *Rosa rugosa* hybrids that were chosen for compact habit, healthy foliage and long season of bloom. Most have proven to be excellent selections. Of the pinks, we have been most attracted to Pierette Pavement. While not a low grower, as many think, this bush is compact and tends to be somewhat wider than high, making it an excellent choice in urban and park situations or for covering banks and such. The medium pink flowers are very large and typically rugose, as is their sweet fragrance. The foliage never shows signs of disease, making it even more attractive where low maintenance is a priority. Rooting cuttings is easy.

POLAREIS

Parentage: unknown, Rosa rugosa *hybrid.*

Nothing stirs the heart of a rose grower quite as much as a new color. When I look at the glistening petals of a Polareis, I can't help but think of a strawberry ice that has had most of the syrup sucked out by a child. The subtlety of color in this new rose is its most attractive trait, while its tantalizing fragrance helps to enhance its charm. This *Rosa rugosa* hybrid has proven very hardy, with foliage that is somewhat textured like its *rugosa* parent but with more gloss. We have seen very little disease on this rose. The bush is well armored with thorns, and the stems are stiff and angular. It propagates readily from cuttings, and we intend to propagate many in the future.

PURPLE PAVEMENT
Parentage: unknown, Rosa rugosa *hybrid.*

This rose is a rapidly spreading plant that is ideal for covering large areas. The leaves are typically rugose with a glossy sheen that reflects this variety's unparalleled healthiness. The flowers are among the deepest colored of the *Rosa rugosa* hybrids, being deep red-purple with shapely unfurling buds. The fragrance is strong and sweet. This rose blooms until late in the season and is easy to root.

RAUBRITTER
Parentage: Rosa macrantha *hybrid.*

This unusual hybrid from the hands of Wilhelm Kordes of Germany is a cross with a species rarely used by breeders, *Rosa macrantha.* It is a bush with thin, lax stems. I have been surprised by the hardiness of this rose, and while blackspot does appear toward the end of summer, it is not overly prone to disease. Its most endearing attributes are the globular form of its small pink flowers and its unique scent, something akin to freshly ground black pepper but without the sneezing. It is one of the latest roses to begin blooming and lasts into early fall. We have found it relatively easy to root.

ROSA MUNDI

(Rosa gallica versicolor)
Parentage: sport of Rosa gallica officinalis.

No two flowers of this rose are ever the same. In a spectacular display of color chaos, each bloom has a different combination of red, pink and white striping. I love to pick dozens of blooms and float them in a large bowl of water, marveling at the uniqueness of each flower. Rosa mundi is one of the harlequins of the rose world. It has enchanted the world since the sixteenth century and, I dare say, will continue to do so for centuries to come.

In order to remain in the horticultural pantheon, a rose has to be tough. Rosa mundi fits the bill. It is among the hardiest of the *Rosa gallica* group and will thrive with little attention for decades. Although not very susceptible to blackspot, this rose will suffer from mildew late in the season. However, I never pay much heed to it as the flowers are usually done by this point and it does not seem to cause the bush undue harm. As with most *gallicas*, the fragrance of Rosa mundi is powerful. It can be easily rooted from cuttings.

SCHNEEZWERG

Parentage: Rosa rugosa × *a Polyantha rose.*

From late spring till hard frost this tough and adaptable bush sends forth innumerable small pure white blossoms. As each semi-double bloom opens, a center of deep yellow stamens adds a cheerful accent to the flower.

Schneezwerg's lustrous, healthy foliage amply demonstrates the disease resistance so common to the *rugosa* roses. The density of this bush makes it a good hedge plant. With annual attention to shaping and thinning, a hedge of Schneezwerg can be a valuable addition to your garden.

To all these attributes, add a sweet and powerful fragrance and a hardiness that is virtually unmatched in the rose world. It is no wonder that Schneezwerg remains one of the most popular white *rugosa* roses, one modern breeders use to create new varieties. Schneezwerg gives you all the beauty of a fresh snowfall without the bother of having to shovel it. This rose is easy to root from softwood cuttings taken just before flowering. Suckers can be used.

SNOW PAVEMENT

Parentage: unknown, Rosa rugosa hybrid.

The color of this rose is white, delicately suffused with lavender, the color of a violet sunset reflecting off snow. This rare pastel is a welcome addition to a garden. At a distance the blooms appear white; it is only when you come closer that the soft coloring becomes apparent. What draws us further into the blossoms is a rich, heady fragrance and unusually long buds that resemble fat, stubby cigars. These expand into very large flowers.

The bush is dense and squat. It spreads rapidly outward, making it an excellent choice for covering banks or other large areas. The foliage is a paragon of health. I know of no healthier foliage in the rose world. The choice of Snow Pavement as an English name is unfortunate as the bush is not a flat ground cover, as the name suggests, and is distinctly more pleasant than asphalt. However, a name is just that. The rose is real, and a name will never do it justice. It is very easy to root.

SUAVEOLENS

Parentage: unknown, Rosa alba *hybrid.*

In the heart of the Balkan mountains of Bulgaria is a steep valley bordering the Tundza River, which eventually spills into the Black Sea. This exotic valley is noteworthy in the history of rose growing, for this is Kazanlik, where the most famous "attar of roses" is made. In early summer the green valley transforms into a pastel carpet as the millions of roses needed to create this famous perfume come into bloom. The aromatic petals are collected and carefully distilled into a substance so highly prized that it was once available only to the nobility of the world. Very few roses contain enough natural fragrance to make

them suitable for the Kazanlik essences. One of these is Kazanlik, a Damask rose named after the town of its origin. Another important variety is the *alba* rose Suaveolens.

Connoisseurs of fragrance should be convinced. Those interested in the beauty of roses will rejoice in the semi-double blooms of nearly pure white surrounding a center of golden yellow stamens. This rose has an informal yet refined look. The bush is quite hardy, healthy and vigorous, and this rose is moderately easy to root. Although not as easy to locate in the nursery trade, this is a rose that you should seek out.

From late spring onward, Stanwell Perpetual produces a regular succession of blush-pink blooms.

9

Low Shrubs

Shrubs growing up to 3 ft. (1 m)

CHAMPLAIN

CHARLES ALBANEL

FRU DAGMAR HASTRUP

HENRY HUDSON

LAMBERT CLOSSE

MORDEN BLUSH

MORDEN RUBY

NICHOLAS

PRAIRIE JOY

ROSE DE MEAUX

ROYAL EDWARD

SIMON FRASER

STANWELL PERPETUAL

STRIPED MOSS

THE FAIRY

TOPAZ JEWEL

TUSCANY & TUSCANY SUPERBA

CHAMPLAIN

Parentage: Rosa kordesii *Wulff* × Rosa laxa × Rosa spinosissima L.

Champlain is a hardy and ever-blooming rose. Once it begins blooming, only the hard frosts can stop it. Although certainly not an ironclad hardy plant, it is a valuable addition to the northern garden. In our garden we often experience a good deal of dieback with Champlain, but we have never lost a plant, and when on its own roots it is able to spring back even if killed to almost ground level.

Champlain is a rich, velvety deep red. In our garden it is definitely the plant people ask about most. In addition to its sumptuous color, this rose is entirely free of disease. It is exceedingly resistant to blackspot and mildew. What is even more exciting is that under outside growing conditions Champlain is virtually free of aphids. Many roses seem somewhat resistant to these pesky green sap suckers, but Champlain is truly exceptional.

Champlain is not a vigorous rose. It is quite low in stature and makes an excellent bedding rose. In fact, if this variety has a fault, it is that the plant seems all bloom at the expense of foliage. With proper pruning, however, it forms a compact and useful garden subject. It is extremely easy to root, although cuttings are often difficult to obtain in numbers due to lack of growth.

CHARLES ALBANEL

Parentage: Rosa rugosa *seedling.*

This rose is very new and virtually unknown in the gardening scene. It is a *rugosa* seedling that is in many ways similar to its relatives, but one that has a special feature that demands attention. It is very dwarfish and spreading and, with time, creates a thick blanket that will smother an embankment or garden bed with its dense foliage and informal, colorful blooms. The height and density of this plant make it one of the most outstanding hardy ground covers available. The new stems are medium green, turning blackish with age, and the branches are quite thorny. The rose hips are medium-sized, orange-red and flattened globular.

The semi-double flowers are a pleasing mauve-red. They begin in early summer and continue until the very end of the season. Many of the more common hardy ground cover roses flower only once, but this new selection from the breeding program at Agriculture Canada creates a living floral carpet throughout the season.

Both the hardiness and disease resistance of this rose are exceptional. It is virtually immune to mildew and blackspot. Given all these attributes, I have no doubt that this variety will become increasingly common in the garden and in public and commercial plantings where masses of low flowering plants are needed. To propagate, take cuttings early in the season just before flowering.

FRU DAGMAR HASTRUP

Parentage: unknown, Rosa rugosa *seedling.*

If there were such a thing as pink spiders that wove cloth, their silken product might resemble the petals of Fru Dagmar Hastrup. The light pink flowers shimmer in the light. They are large and, when opening, resemble chalices. Best of all, they do not stop blooming until freezing temperatures put an end to their prolific beauty. The flowers are intensely fragrant.

This exceedingly hardy rose is a low-growing form and stays fairly compact, becoming more wide than high. It is very well protected by thorns so numerous that there is no smooth stem surface. Both short and somewhat longer thorns are interspersed in this formidable armor. It is a very healthy rose, being nearly immune to blackspot and mildew.

Hips are numerous and large, useful for those growers who enjoy these vitamin-packed fruits.

One of the most endearing qualities of Fru Dagmar Hastrup is its fall foliage. As the daylight hours wane, the green leaves take on a deep maroon tone. The process continues until the foliage changes to deep golden yellow with coppery highlights that seem iridescent. Although I have always enjoyed this rose's blooms in summer, I will never forget the first time I stood transfixed in my garden as the late afternoon sun glanced off the glowing autumn leaves of this petite gem. I still have not found a rose with a more exciting transition into winter. Fru Dagmar Hastrup is fairly easy to root from cuttings, and suckers can be used.

HENRY HUDSON

Parentage: Rosa rugosa *Schneezwerg seedling.*

I have a rare single red peony in my garden. With its ferny foliage, this peony is very beautiful in bloom, but what makes it stand out is the background of snow white Henry Hudson roses, which carpet the ground around it. This low-growing and prolifically blooming plant is another valuable introduction from the Explorer Series of Agriculture Canada.

Henry Hudson has virtually everything you could ask for. Its deep green and copious foliage is free of disease, it is absolutely hardy, its flowers come continuously in wave after wave, it is richly fragrant and its pink-tipped buds open to a sparkling show of white petals. It is truly a northern explorer and an important

addition to the list of hardy roses.

As a low bedding plant this rose is unbeatable, for it maintains a density that few roses can boast, creating a carpet of green that shows off its flowers to good advantage. Be forewarned that, like most *rugosas,* Henry Hudson will spread by suckering, so it is best used where this is desired or where it can be contained. It holds onto its spent blooms, so you may want to pick the old flowers for best appearance. Propagating Henry Hudson from softwood cuttings gives variable results. The best results are with cuttings from early season growth just before flowering. Suckers can be used.

LAMBERT CLOSSE
Parentage: Arthur Bell × John Davis.

Those who feel that shrub roses are unrefined will have to come up with a different excuse to avoid growing this new introduction. The shell pink blooms of Lambert Closse resemble those of the hybrid teas. The petals are pointed, and when the double blooms unfold, the petals reflex outward and create a starlike arrangement that is perfectly symmetrical. The foliage on this small bush is a glossy green and has good resistance to mildew and blackspot, although older leaves will show some. Blossoms appear on this rose throughout the season. It is relatively easy to root, although good cutting wood is scarce because the bush is more flower than leaf. The fragrance of this Canadian Explorer rose is, might I say, refined.

MORDEN BLUSH
Parentage: (Prairie Princess × Morden Amorette) × ((Prairie Princess × (White Bouquet) × (Rosa arkansana × Assiniboine)).

Although I find it a bit tender at my site, I feel it would be unfair not to include this spectacular rose. Even when winterkilled to near the ground, this rose bounces back and produces a wealth of flowers the entire season. And what flowers! The large double blooms are the softest of pinks imaginable and of exquisite form. They possess a faint fragrance. The bush is upright but relatively low in stature. Given a protected site, this rose will reward you with copious clusters of bloom. They are good cut flowers as well. This rose roots easily.

MORDEN RUBY
Parentage: Fire King × (J.W. Fargo × Assiniboine).

Apparently, pixies inhabit my garden. Each time a blossom of Morden Ruby opens, it looks as if they have splashed the deep pink petals with cans of red paint, creating a fascinating spotted pattern that should make many an abstract painter envious. Recently, however, I have learned that the variety released as Morden Ruby was a solid red sport of the spotted original. The plants we originally received were spotted, but some have now sported again to the solid red color, as the photo so clearly shows. It makes me wonder which plant was a sport of which.

Both flowers are beautiful and allow me to forgive the plant's weaknesses. Morden Ruby is rather open, and a severe pruning in spring will help keep the plant denser. It is also a bit too subject to blackspot for my liking. However, a few sprays of sulfur or a blind eye make this all too common weakness disappear. Morden Ruby has an important point in its favor: the blossoms I cherish so highly come in several waves throughout the summer, so I can gaze at these fascinating flowers for many months. Morden Ruby is fairly easy to root, but cuttings often drop leaves shortly after rooting.

NICHOLAS
Parentage: B08 (A15 × D36) × L03 (Rosa kordesii × Applejack).

I was lucky enough to see this rose bloom in my nursery when it was still an unnamed seedling. It had been sent to us by Agriculture Canada as a possible future release in the Explorer program. Little N0-6, as it was then known, immediately caught my attention. The bush is very small, with shiny green foliage that rarely harbors disease. The buds resemble tiny tops, and they spin open to reveal a semidouble flower that is a unique shade of scarlet red. It stays neat and compact and blooms the entire season. It does not have much scent, but its small stature and brilliant color make it a valuable addition to hardy roses. It is very easy to root.

PRAIRIE JOY

Parentage: Prairie Princess × Morden Cardinette.

Some of the earliest improved hardy roses were bred at Agriculture Canada's Morden Research Station in Morden, Manitoba. The strength of these introductions has been superb flower form. Prairie Joy is a newer release that has both excellent form and small stature, making it an ideal low hedge plant. It is a prolific bloomer and has good hardiness. Many of the Morden introductions are prone to blackspot in humid areas. Prairie Joy has better resistance than most of the earlier releases, but we do recommend sulfur sprays to prevent blackspot from marring the otherwise glossy deep green foliage. The semi-double flowers are bright pink and come in clusters till season's end. There is little scent to the blooms. Cuttings root readily.

ROSE DE MEAUX

Parentage: unknown, Rosa centifolia.

Many believe that those of us living in the colder areas are deprived because we cannot grow so many of the beautiful varieties in the rose world. To some extent this is true. We cannot grow the hybrid teas and floribundas, so we are forced to seek out the species and hybrids that will survive in our rigorous climates. Yet this very fact opens up to us a world of roses that those who grow only teas cannot imagine. Roses that can create effects in the garden that are totally unique and exciting. An example of this exhilarating diversity is Rose de Meaux.

The flowers of this rose are not large and splashy but are tight, frilly buttons, a classic rose form in miniature, clear pink and very fragrant. The bush is miniature as well, rarely growing more than 2 ft. (60 cm) high.

Rose de Meaux is considered a temperamental rose, not growing well in poor soils. We are blessed with excellent soil in our garden and have been pleased with the performance of this gem. However, this fact should be a consideration for those working with marginal soils. Certainly the winter has not been a problem. Rose de Meaux has come through our low temperatures unscathed by frost's icy grip, and is also fairly easy to root.

Meaux is a rose we can highlight in the garden, one to cherish for its diminutive elegance and its rare beauty.

ROYAL EDWARD

Parentage: Rosa kordesii × *seedling of complex origin.*

If this rose never bloomed, it would still be a plant worth growing. The small leaves are deepest green and look as though fairies had spent the night waxing and polishing their surfaces. This plant, however, does flower. From early summer till late fall, small acorn-shaped buds unfurl into shapely semi-double blossoms that are elegant in their simplicity. They are a pure pink, devoid of any blue or red shading. Only the most sensitive nose will pick up fragrance from this miniature hybrid. Royal Edward is very easy to root and to grow. Blackspot and mildew are nearly non-existent if the plant is kept well nourished. Few roses can match the healthy glow of this variety. It makes an ideal choice for sites where most low shrub roses would still be too robust.

SIMON FRASER

Parentage: Rosa kordesii *hybrid of complex origin.*

The most common color in roses is pink. There seems no end to the various shades available, yet Simon Fraser has added yet another subtle hue to the pink palette. This pink is somewhere between shrimp and salmon. The blooms themselves are very simple. In fact, the first blooms you see on the bush may be single, but as it matures the number of petals increases to 10 or so. Like other Explorer roses, Simon Fraser has exceedingly healthy foliage and uncommon hardiness. The plant is quite small and boasts one of the most extravagant displays of bloom in its class. Its glossy foliage is nearly hidden by the first flush of bloom in early summer. From then till frost there are always plenty of pink petals to draw attention to this attractive newcomer. Propagators will find this rose easy to root.

STANWELL PERPETUAL

Parentage: Rosa × damascena bifera (*Autumn Damask*) × Rosa spinosissima.

It is by listening to the advice of others that we learn. In one of my correspondences with a rose grower, I was told that I had to acquire the Scotch rose hybrid Stanwell Perpetual. My friend assured me that it would soon become one of my favorites. And so it has.

The Scotch rose has been used to hybridize many roses. Its beauty, hardiness and adaptability to poor growing conditions make it a good breeding parent. Unfortunately, the Scotch rose is an early and one-time bloomer, and most of the hybrids of this variety have inherited this trait. There are a few exceptions, and the Stanwell Perpetual is, in my opinion, the very best of them. This rose was a cross with the exotically fragrant and long-blooming Autumn Damask. It inherited the tremendous hardiness and toughness of its Scotch parent and the fragrant double blooms of its Damask parent. Best of all, it inherited the ability of Autumn Damask to flower throughout the season.

The flower is double, with the old-time charm of the Damask rose. Its soft, blush-pink blossoms cover the plant in late spring, and from then on a regular procession of flowers appears on this gracefully arching low bush. The foliage is a very deep green and, aside from a natural purplish discoloration, is unmarred by disease. It is fairly easy to root, but is usually budded or grafted. If on its own roots, it will eventually produce suckers that can be used.

Stanwell Perpetual never fails to make me stop, bend down and smell the roses. It asks very little of us and gives so much. It pays to take advice.

STRIPED MOSS

Parentage: unknown, Rosa centifolia muscosa.

Humans seem to crave the unusual in nature. In the gardening world we raise curious dwarfs, plants with twisted stems and foliage, and trees and shrubs with oddly colored foliage and flowers. So it is that roses such as Striped Moss are still found growing in our gardens, for this is, indeed, an odd rose.

The flowers are double, cupped and open flat. The white petals, streaked with random stripes of deep and lighter pink, create an effect both startling and intriguing. Among the striped roses, Striped Moss is one of the hardiest, reasonably easy to root, and therefore of interest to northern growers; however it is subject to blackspot. It is also blessed with a good fragrance and the interesting fuzziness associated with the Moss roses.

The bush is small, upright, with stems and buds well mossed, and is well suited to an intimate corner in the garden where the sun can warm its branches and give brilliance to the blossoms of this lovable oddity.

THE FAIRY

Parentage: Paul Crampel × Lady Gay.

The miniature roses (hybrids of *Rosa polyantha*) hold a special place in the rose world. Their diminutive stature, accompanied by their prolific flowering ability, make them highly sought-after as pot plants and edging plants. Unfortunately for northern gardeners, most of the miniatures are tender and cannot survive outdoors in cold climates. There are a few exceptions, and one of the most notable is one of the older miniatures.

The Fairy is still popular because it is a beautiful soft pink color and, once in bloom, is never out of bloom till it freezes. Another reason is the tenacity of this small plant. It survives where others wither and die. When exposed to temperatures below −22°F (−30°C) without snow cover, the stems may kill back to near the ground, but even in these situations the root system will send up new shoots in the spring. Given a protected site, The Fairy will provide years of satisfaction. The tiny double blooms come in clusters so prolific that the bush resembles a giant bouquet. Although it is generally healthy, you can expect some blackspot in humid areas, so you may want to consider sprays of sulfur to prevent infection. The Fairy is easy to root from cuttings.

TOPAZ JEWEL

Parentage: Golden Angel × Belle Poitvine.

It is interesting that in China yellow roses are associated with lewd and immoral behavior and are generally unwanted in gardens. In North America yellow symbolizes friendship and is among the most sought-after colors in roses. I will enjoy the yellow tones of Topaz Jewel without ascribing any human values to the lemony quality of its flowers. Although our plants kill back in severe winters, this repeat-flowering rose will still produce blowsy semi-double blooms from pointed buds that have a characteristic vertical orange stripe. When open, they have a deliciously fruity and subtle fragrance. The stems of this rose are rigid and angular, with vicious hooked thorns. The medium green leaves are somewhat prone to blackspot, but if the plant is healthy, this is not a serious problem. Sprays of sulfur will prevent infection. Rooting success with Topaz Jewel varies, the best crops being produced when cuttings are collected early in the season.

TUSCANY & TUSCANY SUPERBA

Parentage: unknown, Rosa gallica *hybrid.*

Planting many of the shrub roses is akin to starting a raspberry patch. Roses are, after all, a type of bramble. They spread by underground roots that run outward and pop up several feet from where they started. Older canes will often die out to be replaced by new suckers. If you dig up roses, you will frequently be shocked at the lack of roots supporting the tops. There are often very few fibrous roots.

Tuscany superba is a low suckering plant in this vein, but the blossoms on these suckers are as decorative as the finest velvet. The surface of the petals appears soft and is a purple as rich and deep as a royal robe. These same petals are also richly endowed with superb perfume. This rose is one of the very hardiest of the *Rosa gallica* group, and is also one of the oldest, having been cherished by nobleman and commoner for centuries. The superba type is a find from the early nineteenth century and differs only in a slightly more symmetrical form and a few more petals.

Unlike many ground-cover roses, Charles Albanel creates a floral carpet until the end of the season.

10

Ground Covers

Procumbent or ground-hugging shrubs

MAX GRAF

ROSA PAULII

MAX GRAF

Parentage: Rosa rugosa × Rosa wichuraiana.

This rose is vitally important in the historical development of many of our newest and best hardy shrub roses. Discovered in Connecticut by James Bowditch, this rose came to the attention of Wilhelm Kordes of Germany. He saved seed from a chance fruit on his bush and the seedling that resulted had good hardiness and a remarkable resistance to disease. He named it *Rosa kordesii*. Subsequent crosses using this new species resulted in many important hardy, healthy varieties. Later, the breeder Felicitas Svejda of Canada also used these descendants of Max Graf to introduce blackspot resistance into the Explorer Series of roses.

Although not commonly seen in gardens, the original Max Graf can be useful to the northern gardener, for not only is it hardy and healthy, it also has a low branching structure that makes it a good ground cover. Its lax stems stretch outward, bending down from their own weight. As each successive layer covers the previous layers, a fairly dense low bush is created that is attractive and effective.

Because the flower is single and nonrecurrent, we should not dismiss it. Surrounding a prominent center of deep yellow stamens are five petals of clear, satiny pink that are delightfully scented. Even when not in flower, however, the healthy sheen of the leaves and the long, arching, fresh-green branches add beauty and texture to the garden. Max Graf is very easy to root from cuttings and will also layer well.

ROSA PAULII

Parentage: unknown, supposed to be Rosa arvensis × Rosa rugosa.

A fascinating rose and one of the only true creeping roses that can be grown in the north. For me, this rose was an interesting lesson in the differences between budded and own-rooted plants. When I first received Rosa paulii it was budded onto *Rosa multiflora* roots. I grew it the first year and was disappointed that it was not a true ground cover as I had hoped. It seemed to grow upward and then gradually arch outward. I did, however, instruct the propagator to take cuttings. The next summer I was walking through the beds and came upon what looked like sinuous, thorny snakes on the ground. I had never seen a rose like it. I quickly backtracked to the sign and could hardly believe that this was the same plant that I had brought in. The *multiflora* root had caused the plant to thrust upward, whereas these own-rooted plants never left the soil's surface. The two plants, alike in every respect but their roots, behaved in two completely different manners. This difference points to the importance of knowing what kind of plant you have, for their growth pattern can be significantly altered by placing them on a rootstock.

While this rose does not attain any height, it certainly does not lack vigor. It will grow several feet a year and will rapidly fill a good-sized area with its long, snaky shoots. In the early summer the healthy and heavily textured foliage forms large buds, which open to immense pure white single blooms. The narrower than usual petals converge in the center where a sunburst of golden stamens completes the simple beauty of this flower with delicate elegance. The rose's sweet fragrance and colorful display of yellow and orange foliage in the fall help to make up for the fleeting season of this most useful plant. It roots and layers easily.

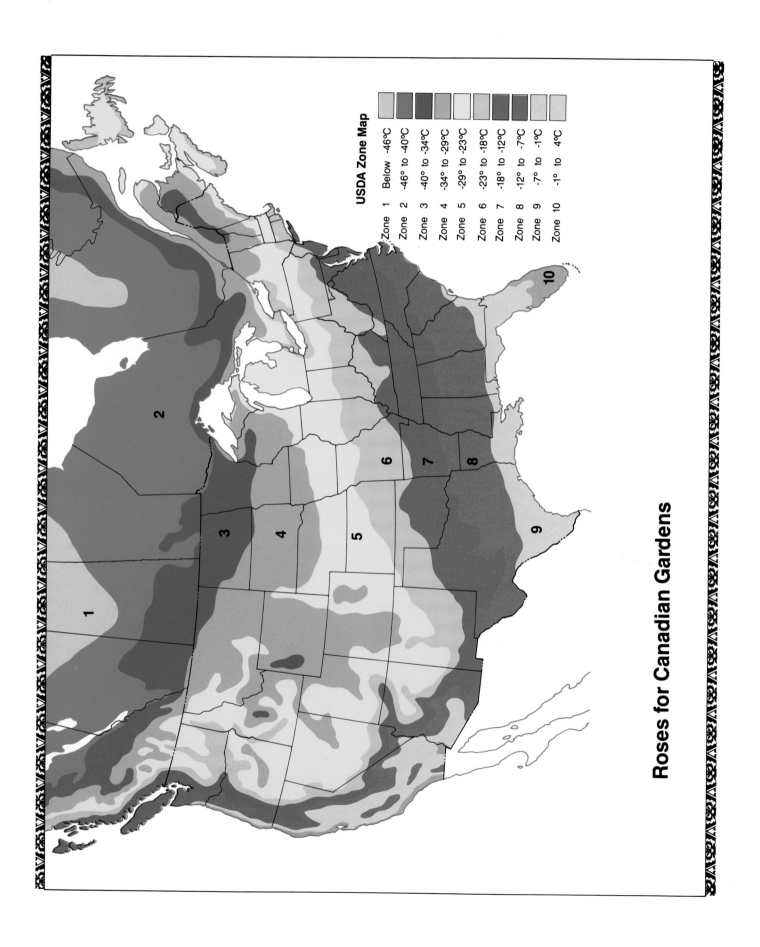

USDA Zone Map

Zone 1 Below -46°C
Zone 2 -46° to -40°C
Zone 3 -40° to -34°C
Zone 4 -34° to -29°C
Zone 5 -29° to -23°C
Zone 6 -23° to -18°C
Zone 7 -18° to -12°C
Zone 8 -12° to -7°C
Zone 9 -7° to -1°C
Zone 10 -1° to 4°C

Roses for Canadian Gardens

List of
Hardy Varieties

The following varieties are those believed sufficiently hardy to be grown in Zones 2 to 5. The varieties chosen are those that are currently available in the nursery trade. There are countless other roses, many of excellent quality and value, but they are either difficult or impossible to obtain. I have relied upon the expertise of others to assign each variety to a species or category. Some roses might just as easily be put in other sections, as they are often the result of interspecific breeding and have characteristics common to both species. The designation of color, form, vigor, fragrance and blooming time are from the results of my own observations and those of others in the field. Some of these are somewhat subjective, and differences may occur according to where a variety is grown and the care given to it. Hardiness designations are based on observation, information from reliable sources and a bit of educated guesswork. These hardiness ratings should be used merely as a guide to assist those choosing suitable roses for their area.

THE VARIETIES	COLOR	FORM	HARDINESS ZONE	VIGOR	FRAGRANCE	SEASON	SUITABILITY FOR HEDGING	DISEASE SUSCEPTIBILITY	BREEDER	ORIGIN	INTRODUCED
ROSA ACICULARIS											
Dornroschen	dp	d	5	sv	ff	r		BS-2	Kordes	Germany	1960
ROSA ALBA											
Amelia	mp	sd	3-4	sv	fff	s	H	BS-1	Vibert	France	1823
Belle Amour	lp	d	3-4	v	ff	s	H	BS-1	seedling	France	c. 1940
Blanche de Belgique	w	d	3-4	v	fff	s	H	BS-1	Vibert	France	1817
Blush hip	lp	d	3-4	v	fff	s		BS-1	unknown	UK	1840
Celestial (*Celeste*)	lp	d	3-4	v	fff	s	H	BS-0	unknown	unknown	old
Chloris (*Rosée du Matin*)	lp	d	3-4	v	ff	s	H	BS-0	unknown	unknown	old
Félicité Parmentier	lp	vd	3-4	sv	fff	s	H	BS-1	unknown	unknown	1834
Jeanne d'Arc	w	d	3-4	v	fff	s	H	BS-1	Vibert	France	1818
Königin von Dänemark (*Queen of Denmark*)	mp	vd	3-4	sv	fff	s	H	BS-0	unknown	unknown	1826

COLOR
w=white or nearly white
p/w=pink and white
pb=pink blend
p/y=pink and yellow
lp=light pink
mp=medium pink
dp=deep pink
mr=medium red
dr=deep red
rb=red blend
m=mauve
mb=mauve blend
ly=light yellow
my=medium yellow
dy=deep yellow
yo=yellow-orange
o=orange
or=orange-red
yo=yellow-orange
c/s=coppery salmon

FORM
s=single
s+=slightly more than single
sd=semi-double
d=double
vd=very double or quartered

HARDINESS ZONE
2 to 5 (see Zone map)

VIGOR
g=ground cover
l=low
sv=semi-vigorous
v=vigorous
cl=climber

FRAGRANCE
f=little or no fragrance
ff=moderate fragrance
fff=exceptional fragrance

SEASON
sp=spring
s=summer
r=repeating
c=continuous bloomer

SUITABILITY FOR HEDGING
H

DISEASE SUSCEPTIBILITY
Blackspot:
BS-0= Immune or so little as to be insignificant.
BS-1= Noticeable but generally affecting fewer than 25% of leaves.
BS-2= Affecting at least 50% of leaves, some defoliation without protection.
BS-3= Affecting most of leaves, heavy defoliation without protection.

Mildew:
M=Varieties that are particularly susceptible to mildew.

Rust:
R= Varieties that are particularly susceptible to rust.

Note: Although roses are subject to several diseases, by far the most important disease of hardy varieties is blackspot. Those in drier climates may not have problems with blackspot, but in more humid areas blackspot can seriously affect many roses. These designations are based on the incidence of blackspot in a moderately humid site. Although you may find the incidence of blackspot either more or less severe than indicated by these ratings, they at least will offer a relative scale of blackspot susceptibility.

THE VARIETIES	COLOR	FORM	HARDINESS ZONE	VIGOR	FRAGRANCE	SEASON	SUITABILITY FOR HEDGING	DISEASE SUSCEPTIBILITY	BREEDER	ORIGIN	INTRODUCED
Maiden's Blush Great (*Rosa alba incarnata*)	lp	vd	3-4	sv	fff	s	H	BS-1	unknown	unknown	*c.* 1400
Maiden's Blush Small	lp	vd	3-4	l	fff	s	H	BS-1	Kew Gardens	UK	1797
Maxima	w	d	3-4	v	fff	s		BS-0	unknown	?	*c.* 1680
Minette	lp	d	3-4	sv	fff	s	H	BS-0	unknown	France?	1819
Mme. Plantier	w	vd	3-4	v	fff	s		BS-1	Plantier	France	1835
Pompon Blanc Parfait	w	vd	3-4	sv	fff	s		BS-1	unknown	unknown	*c.* 1876
Semi-plena	w	sd	3-4	v	fff	s		BS-1	unknown	Europe	*c.* 1500
Suaveolens	w	sd	3-4	v	fff	s		BS-0	unknown	Europe	*c.* 1500
ROSA BEGGERIANA											
Mrs. John McNab	w	sd	3	sv	ff	s		BS-0	Skinner	Canada	1941
Polstjarnan	w	s	2	v	f	s		BS-0	Wasa	Finland	1937
ROSA BLANDA											
Betty Bland	dp	d	2	v	ff	s		BS-1	Skinner	Canada	1926
ROSA CENTIFOLIA											
A Longs Pédoncules	lp	d	4	sv	ff	s		BS-1	Robert	France	1854
Blanche fleur	w	d	4	sv	fff	s		BS-1	Vibert	France	1835
Blush Moss	lp	d	4	sv	fff	s		BS-1	unknown	unknown	*c.* 1844
Bullata (*Lettuce leafed rose*)	dp	d	4	sv	fff	s		BS-1	unknown	unknown	*c.* 1500
Célina	dp	sd	4	sv	ff	s		BS-1	Hardy	France	1855
Common Moss (*Old Pink Moss*), (*Communis*)	mp	d	4	sv	fff	s		BS-1	unknown	France	1696

THE VARIETIES	COLOR	FORM	HARDINESS ZONE	VIGOR	FRAGRANCE	SEASON	SUITABILITY FOR HEDGING	DISEASE SUSCEPTIBILITY	BREEDER	ORIGIN	INTRODUCED
Crested Moss (*R. centifolia cristata*), (*Chapeau de Napoléon*)	dp	d	4	sv	fff	s		BS-1	Vibert	France	1826
Crimson Moss	dr	d	4	sv	ff	s		BS-1	Lee	UK	*c.* 1846
Fantin-Latour	mp	vd	4	sv	fff	s		BS-1	unknown	unknown	?
Henri Martin	mr	d	4	sv	ff	s		BS-1	Laffay	France	1863
Hunslett Moss	dp	d	4	l	fff	s		BS-1	Brooke	UK	1984
Jeanne de Monfort	mp	d	4	sv	fff	s		BS-1	Robert	France	1851
La Noblesse	lp	vd	4	sv	fff	s		BS-1	unknown	unknown	1856
Marie de Blois	mp	d	4	sv	fff	c		BS-1	Robert	France	1852
Mme. William Paul	pb	d	4	l	ff	r		BS-2	Paul	UK	1869
Nuits de Young (*Old Black Moss*)	rb	d	4	sv	ff	s	H	BS-2	Laffay	France	1845
Paul Ricault	dp	vd	4	sv	fff	s		BS-1	Portemer	France	1845
Quatre Saisons Blanc Mousseaux (*Perpetual White Moss*)	w	d	4	sv	ff	s		BS-1	Laffay	France	*c.* 1848
Rose de Meaux	mp	vd	4	l	fff	s		BS-2	Sweet	UK	*c.* 1789

COLOR
w=white or nearly white
p/w=pink and white
pb=pink blend
p/y=pink and yellow
lp=light pink
mp=medium pink
dp=deep pink
mr=medium red
dr=deep red
rb=red blend
m=mauve
mb=mauve blend
ly=light yellow
my=medium yellow
dy=deep yellow
yo=yellow-orange
o=orange
or=orange-red
yo=yellow-orange
c/s=coppery salmon

FORM
s=single
s+=slightly more than single
sd=semi-double
d=double
vd=very double or quartered

HARDINESS ZONE
2 to 5 (see Zone map)

VIGOR
g=ground cover
l=low
sv=semi-vigorous
v=vigorous
cl=climber

FRAGRANCE
f=little or no fragrance
ff=moderate fragrance
fff=exceptional fragrance

SEASON
sp=spring
s=summer
r=repeating
c=continuous bloomer

SUITABILITY FOR HEDGING
H

DISEASE SUSCEPTIBILITY
Blackspot:
BS-0= Immune or so little as to be insignificant.
BS-1= Noticeable but generally affecting fewer than 25% of leaves.
BS-2= Affecting at least 50% of leaves, some defoliation without protection.
BS-3= Affecting most of leaves, heavy defoliation without protection.

Mildew:
M=Varieties that are particularly susceptible to mildew.

Rust:
R= Varieties that are particularly susceptible to rust.

Note: Although roses are subject to several diseases, by far the most important disease of hardy varieties is blackspot. Those in drier climates may not have problems with blackspot, but in more humid areas blackspot can seriously affect many roses. These designations are based on the incidence of blackspot in a moderately humid site. Although you may find the incidence of blackspot either more or less severe than indicated by these ratings, they at least will offer a relative scale of blackspot susceptibility.

THE VARIETIES	COLOR	FORM	HARDINESS ZONE	VIGOR	FRAGRANCE	SEASON	SUITABILITY FOR HEDGING	DISEASE SUSCEPTIBILITY	BREEDER	ORIGIN	INTRODUCED
Souvenir de Pierre Vibert	pb	d	4	sv	ff	r		BS-1	Morseau-Robert	France	1867
Spong	mp	d	4	sv	ff	s	H	BS-1	Spong	France	1805
Striped Moss	p/w	d	4	l	ff	s		BS-2	unknown	unknown	?
The Bishop	m	vd	4	sv	ff	s		BS-1	unknown	unknown	?
Tour de Malakoff (*Black Jack*)	mb	d	4	v	ff	s		BS-1	Soupert & Notting	Luxem.	1856
Violacée	mb	d	4	sv	ff	s		BS-1	Soupert & Notting	Luxem.	1876
White Bath	w	d	4	sv	fff	s		BS-1	Salter	UK	1817
William Lobb (*Old Velvet Moss*)	mb	d	4	v	ff	s		BS-1	Laffay	France	1855
ROSA CINNOMOMEA											
Plena	mp	d	3	sv	fff	s	H	BS-0	unknown	unknown	*c.* 1596
ROSA EGLANTERIA											
Amy Robsart	dp	s	4	v	ff	s	H	BS-3	Penzance	UK	1894
Goldbusch	my	sd	4	v	ff	s	H	BS-1	Kordes	Germany	1954
Greenmantle	r	s	4	v	ff	s	H	BS-3	Penzance	UK	1894
Hebe's Lip (*Rubrotincta*), (*Reine Blanche*)	w	s	4	sv	ff	s	H	BS-2	Paul	UK	1912
Herbstfeuer (*Autumn Fire*)	dr	sd	4	v	f	r	H	BS-1	Kordes	Germany	1961
Julia Mannering	lp	s	4	v	ff	s	H	BS-2	Penzance	UK	1895
La Belle Distinguée (*Scarlet Sweetbriar*), (*La Petite Duchesse*)	dr	d	4	sv	f	s	H	BS-2	unknown	unknown	?
Lady Penzance	p/y	s	4	v	ff	s	H	BS-3	Penzance	UK	1894
Lord Penzance	p/y	s	4	v	ff	s	H	BS-3	Penzance	UK	1890

THE VARIETIES	COLOR	FORM	HARDINESS ZONE	VIGOR	FRAGRANCE	SEASON	SUITABILITY FOR HEDGING	DISEASE SUSCEPTIBILITY	BREEDER	ORIGIN	INTRODUCED
Manning's Blush	w	d	4	sv	ff	s	H	BS-2	unknown	unknown	c. 1800
Meg Merrilees'	dr	sd	4	v	ff	s	H	BS-3	Penzance	UK	c. 1894
ROSA FOETIDA											
Austrian Copper	or	s	3-4	sv	f	s		BS-3	unknown	Asia	c. 1500
Lawrence Johnston	dy	sd	5	cl	ff	r		BS-3	Pernet-Ducher	France	1923
Persian Yellow	dy	d	3-4	sv	f	s		BS-3	unknown	S.W. Asia	1837
Soleil d'Or	yo	d	4-5	sv	fff	r		BS-3	Pernet-Ducher	France	1900
ROSA GALLICA											
Agatha (*Agathe*)	dp	sd	3-4	sv	ff	s		BS-1	unknown	Europe	?
Alain Blanchard	rb	sd	4	sv	ff	s		BS-1	Vibert	France	1839
Alika (*Gallica grandiflora*)	mr	sd	3-4	v	fff	s		BS-1	Hanson	?	1906

COLOR
w=white or nearly white
p/w=pink and white
pb=pink blend
p/y=pink and yellow
lp=light pink
mp=medium pink
dp=deep pink
mr=medium red
dr=deep red
rb=red blend
m=mauve
mb=mauve blend
ly=light yellow
my=medium yellow
dy=deep yellow
yo=yellow-orange
o=orange
or=orange-red
yo=yellow-orange
c/s=coppery salmon

FORM
s=single
s+=slightly more than single
sd=semi-double
d=double
vd=very double or quartered

HARDINESS ZONE
2 to 5 (see Zone map)

VIGOR
g=ground cover
l=low
sv=semi-vigorous
v=vigorous
cl=climber

FRAGRANCE
f=little or no fragrance
ff=moderate fragrance
fff=exceptional fragrance

SEASON
sp=spring
s=summer
r=repeating
c=continuous bloomer

SUITABILITY FOR HEDGING
H

DISEASE SUSCEPTIBILITY
Blackspot:
BS-0= Immune or so little as to be insignificant.
BS-1= Noticeable but generally affecting fewer than 25% of leaves.
BS-2= Affecting at least 50% of leaves, some defoliation without protection.
BS-3= Affecting most of leaves, heavy defoliation without protection.

Mildew:
M=Varieties that are particularly susceptible to mildew.

Rust:
R= Varieties that are particularly susceptible to rust.

Note: Although roses are subject to several diseases, by far the most important disease of hardy varieties is blackspot. Those in drier climates may not have problems with blackspot, but in more humid areas blackspot can seriously affect many roses. These designations are based on the incidence of blackspot in a moderately humid site. Although you may find the incidence of blackspot either more or less severe than indicated by these ratings, they at least will offer a relative scale of blackspot susceptibility.

THE VARIETIES	COLOR	FORM	HARDINESS ZONE	VIGOR	FRAGRANCE	SEASON	SUITABILITY FOR HEDGING	DISEASE SUSCEPTIBILITY	BREEDER	ORIGIN	INTRODUCED
Anaïs Ségalas	rb	d	4	l	fff	s		BS-1	Vibert	France	1837
Antonia d'Ormois	lp	d	4	sv	ff	s		BS-1	Roseraie de l'Hay	France	?
Apothecary's Rose (*Rosa gallica officinalis*)	dp	sd	4	sv	fff	s		BS-1	unknown	unknown	*c.* 1600
Assemblage des Beautés (*Rouge Eblouissante*)	dr	vd	4	sv	ff	s		BS-1	unknown	France	*c.* 1823
Belle de Crécy	mb	d	4	sv	ff	s		BS-1	unknown	unknown	*c.* 1850
Belle Isis	lp	vd	4	l	fff	s		BS-1	Parmentier	Belgium	1845
Camaieux	p/w	vd	4	l	ff	s		BS-1	Vibert	France	1830
Cardinal de Richelieu	mb	vd	4	l	ff	s		BS-1	Laffay	France	1840
Charles de Mills	rb	vd	4	sv	fff	s		BS-1	Roseraie de l'Hay	France	old
Complicata	mp	s	4-5	v	ff	s		BS-1	unknown	unknown	old
Comte de Nanteuil	mb	d	4	sv	ff	s		BS-1	Roeser	France	1834
Comtesse de Lacépède	w	vd	4	sv	ff	s		BS-1	unknown	France	1840
Conditorum	dr	sd	4	sv	fff	s		BS-1	unknown	France	old
Cosimo Ridolfi	mb	vd	4	l	ff	s		BS-1	Vibert	France	1842
Cramoisi Picoté	rb	vd	4	l	f	s		BS-1	Vibert	France	1834
D'Agnesseau	dr	vd	4	sv	ff	s		BS-1	Vibert	France	1823
Duc de Fitzjames	mb	vd	4	sv	ff	s		BS-1	unknown	unknown	*c.* 1885
Duc de Guiche	rb	d	4	sv	fff	s		BS-1	Prévost	France	1835
Duchesse d'Angoulême (*Duc d'Angoulême*)	lp	vd	4	sv	fff	s		BS-1	Vibert	France	*c.* 1835
Duchesse de Buccleugh	rb	vd	4	v	ff	s		BS-1	Robert	France	1860
Duchesse de Montebello	lp	vd	4	sv	fff	s		BS-1	Laffay	France	1829

THE VARIETIES	COLOR	FORM	HARDINESS ZONE	VIGOR	FRAGRANCE	SEASON	SUITABILITY FOR HEDGING	DISEASE SUSCEPTIBILITY	BREEDER	ORIGIN	INTRODUCED
George Vibert	pb	d	4	sv	ff	s		BS-1	Robert	France	1853
Gloire de France	lp	vd	4	l	ff	s		BS-2	unknown	unknown	c. 1819
Gros Provins Panaché	mb	d	4	sv	fff	s		BS-1	unknown	unknown	?
Henri Fouquier	mp	vd	4	l	fff	s		BS-1	unknown	unknown	1854
Hippolyte	mb	vd	4	v	ff	s		BS-1	unknown	unknown	c. 1820
Ipsilanté	pb	v	4	sv	fff	s		BS-1	unknown	unknown	1821
James Mason	dr	sd	4	sv	ff	s		BS-1	Beales	UK	1982
Jenny Duval	mb	sd	4	sv	fff	s		BS-1,M	unknown	unknown	c. 1750
La Belle Sultane (Violacea)	mb	sd	4	v	ff	s		BS-1	unknown	unknown	1795
La Plus Belle des Ponctuées	pb	vd	4	v	ff	s		BS-1	unknown	unknown	?
Nestor	pb	d	4	sv	ff	s		BS-1	unknown	unknown	c. 1846
Oeillet Flamand	pb	vd	4	sv	ff	s		BS-1	Vibert	France	1845
Oeillet Parfait	w	vd	4	v	ff	s		BS-0	Foulard	France	1841
Ombrée Parfaite	pb	vd	4	l	ff	s		BS-1	Vibert	France	1823

COLOR
w=white or nearly white
p/w=pink and white
pb=pink blend
p/y=pink and yellow
lp=light pink
mp=medium pink
dp=deep pink
mr=medium red
dr=deep red
rb=red blend
m=mauve
mb=mauve blend
ly=light yellow
my=medium yellow
dy=deep yellow
yo=yellow-orange
o=orange
or=orange-red
yo=yellow-orange
c/s=coppery salmon

FORM
s=single
s+=slightly more than single
sd=semi-double
d=double
vd=very double or quartered

HARDINESS ZONE
2 to 5 (see Zone map)

VIGOR
g=ground cover
l=low
sv=semi-vigorous
v=vigorous
cl=climber

FRAGRANCE
f=little or no fragrance
ff=moderate fragrance
fff=exceptional fragrance

SEASON
sp=spring
s=summer
r=repeating
c=continuous bloomer

SUITABILITY FOR HEDGING
H

DISEASE SUSCEPTIBILITY
Blackspot:
BS-0= Immune or so little as to be insignificant.
BS-1= Noticeable but generally affecting fewer than 25% of leaves.
BS-2= Affecting at least 50% of leaves, some defoliation without protection.
BS-3= Affecting most of leaves, heavy defoliation without protection.

Mildew:
M=Varieties that are particularly susceptible to mildew.

Rust:
R= Varieties that are particularly susceptible to rust.

Note: Although roses are subject to several diseases, by far the most important disease of hardy varieties is blackspot. Those in drier climates may not have problems with blackspot, but in more humid areas blackspot can seriously affect many roses. These designations are based on the incidence of blackspot in a moderately humid site. Although you may find the incidence of blackspot either more or less severe than indicated by these ratings, they at least will offer a relative scale of blackspot susceptibility.

THE VARIETIES	COLOR	FORM	HARDINESS ZONE	VIGOR	FRAGRANCE	SEASON	SUITABILITY FOR HEDGING	DISEASE SUSCEPTIBILITY	BREEDER	ORIGIN	INTRODUCED
Perle de Panachées	p/w	d	4	v	ff	s		BS-1	Vibert	France	1845
Président de Sèze (*Mme. Hébert*)	pb	vd	4	sv	ff	s		BS-1	unknown	unknown	c. 1836
Rosa Mundi (*R. gallica versicolor*)	p/w	d	4	sv	ff	s		BS-1	unknown	unknown	c. 1580
Rose du Maître d'Ecole	dp	v	4	l	ff	s		BS-1	Miellez	France	1840
Sissinghurst Castle (*Rose des Maures*)	dr	vd	4	l	ff	s		BS-1	unknown	unknown	old
Surpasse Tout	rb	vd	4	sv	ff	s		BS-1	unknown	unknown	c. 1832
Tricolore (*Reine Marguerite*)	dp	vd	4	sv	ff	s		BS-1	Lahaye Père	France	1827
Tricolore de Flandre	pb	vd	4	sv	ff	s		BS-1	Van Houtte	Belgium	1846
Tuscany (*Old Velvet Rose*)	rb	d	4	sv	ff	s		BS-1	unknown	unknown	?
Tuscany Superb	rb	d	4	sv	ff	s		BS-2	Paul	UK	1848
ROSA GLAUCA											
Carmenetta	mp	s	2	v	f	s		BS-0	Agr. Canada	Canada	1923
ROSA MOYESSI											
Eddie's Crimson	dr	d	4	v	f	s		BS-1	Eddie	Canada	1956
Eddie's Jewel	mr	d	4	v	f	r		BS-1	Eddie	Canada	1962
Fred Streeter	dp	s	4	v	f	s		BS-1	Jackman	UK	1951
Geranium	or	s	3-4	v	f	s		BS-0	Royal Hort. Soc.	UK	1938
Highodensis	dp	s	3-4	v	f	s		BS-0	Hillier	UK	1928
Marguerite Hilling	mp	s+	5	v	f	r		BS-1	Hillier	UK	1959
Nevada	w	s+	5	v	f	r		BS-1	Dot	Spain	1927
ROSA NITIDA											
Aylsham	dp	d	3	l	f	s		BS-0	Wright	Canada	1948

THE VARIETIES	COLOR	FORM	HARDINESS ZONE	VIGOR	FRAGRANCE	SEASON	SUITABILITY FOR HEDGING	DISEASE SUSCEPTIBILITY	BREEDER	ORIGIN	INTRODUCED
Defender	dp	s	2-3	sv	ff	s		BS-0	Darthuis	Holland	1971
Métis	mp	d	2-3	sv	ff	s	H	BS-0	Simonet	Canada	1967
ROSA POLYANTHA											
The Fairy	lp	d	4-5	l	f	c		BS-1	Bentall	UK	1932
ROSA RUBRIFOLIA (*GLAUCA*)											
Carmenetta	mp	s	2	v	f	s		BS-0	Agr. Canada	Canada	1923
ROSA RUGOSA											
Agnes	my	d	3	sv	fff	r	H	BS-0	Saunders	Canada	1922
Amelie Gravereaux	rb	d	3	v	fff	r	H	BS-0	Gravereaux	France	1903
Belle Poitvine	mp	sd	4	sv	ff	r	H	BS-0	Bruant	France	1984

COLOR
w=white or nearly white
p/w=pink and white
pb=pink blend
p/y=pink and yellow
lp=light pink
mp=medium pink
dp=deep pink
mr=medium red
dr=deep red
rb=red blend
m=mauve
mb=mauve blend
ly=light yellow
my=medium yellow
dy=deep yellow
yo=yellow-orange
o=orange
or=orange-red
yo=yellow-orange
c/s=coppery salmon

FORM
s=single
s+=slightly more than single
sd=semi-double
d=double
vd=very double or quartered

HARDINESS ZONE
2 to 5 (see Zone map)

VIGOR
g=ground cover
l=low
sv=semi-vigorous
v=vigorous
cl=climber

FRAGRANCE
f=little or no fragrance
ff=moderate fragrance
fff=exceptional fragrance

SEASON
sp=spring
s=summer
r=repeating
c=continuous bloomer

SUITABILITY FOR HEDGING
H

DISEASE SUSCEPTIBILITY
Blackspot:
BS-0= Immune or so little as to be insignificant.
BS-1= Noticeable but generally affecting fewer than 25% of leaves.
BS-2= Affecting at least 50% of leaves, some defoliation without protection.
BS-3= Affecting most of leaves, heavy defoliation without protection.

Mildew:
M=Varieties that are particularly susceptible to mildew.

Rust:
R= Varieties that are particularly susceptible to rust.

Note: Although roses are subject to several diseases, by far the most important disease of hardy varieties is blackspot. Those in drier climates may not have problems with blackspot, but in more humid areas blackspot can seriously affect many roses. These designations are based on the incidence of blackspot in a moderately humid site. Although you may find the incidence of blackspot either more or less severe than indicated by these ratings, they at least will offer a relative scale of blackspot susceptibility.

THE VARIETIES	COLOR	FORM	HARDINESS ZONE	VIGOR	FRAGRANCE	SEASON	SUITABILITY FOR HEDGING	DISEASE SUSCEPTIBILITY	BREEDER	ORIGIN	INTRODUCED
Blanc Double de Coubert	w	sd	2-3	v	fff	r	H	BS-0	Cochet-Cochet	France	1892
Carmen	dr	s	4	sv	ff	r	H	BS-1	Lambert	Germany	1907
Charles Albanel	m	sd	2-3	g	ff	c		BS-0	Svejda	Canada	1982
Conrad Ferdinand Meyer	mp	d	4-5	v	fff	r	H	BS-2,R	Müller	Germany	1899
Culverbrae	dr	vd	4	sv	ff	r	H	BS-0	Gobbee	UK	1973
Dart's Dash	m	sd	2-3	sv	fff	c	H	BS-0,M	unknown	unknown	?
David Thompson	dp	d	2-3	sv	ff	c	H	BS-0	Svejda	Canada	1979
Delicata	mp	sd	3	sv	ff	r	H	BS-0	Cooling	?	1898
Dr. Eckener	p/y	sd	5	v	fff	r		BS-1	Berger	Germany	1930
Dwarf Pavement	mp	sd	2-3	sv	fff	r	H	BS-0	Uhl	Germany	?
Fimbriata	lp	sd	4	sv	f	r	H	BS-0	Morlet	France	1891
F.J. Grootendorst	mr	d	3-4	v	f	c	H	BS-1	De Goey or Skinner	Holland Canada	1918 1908
Foxi Pavement	dp	sd	2-3	sv	fff	r	H	BS-0	Uhl	Germany	?
Fru Dagmar Hastrup (*Fru Dagmar Hartopp*)	mp	s	2-3	l	fff	c		BS-0	Hastrup	Denmark	1914
George Will	dp	d	2-3	sv	fff	r		BS-1	Skinner	Canada	1939
Grootendorst supreme	dr	d	3-4	v	f	c	H	BS-1	Grootendorst	Holland	1936
Hansa	m	d	3	v	fff	r	H	BS-0	Schaum & Van Tol	Holland	1905
Henry Hudson	w	d	2-3	l	fff	c		BS-0	Svejda	Canada	1961
Hunter	dr	d	4	sv	fff	c		BS-1	Mattock	UK	1961
Jens Munk	mp	sd	2-3	sv	ff	c	H	BS-0	Svejda	Canada	1974
Lady Curzon	lp	s	4	sv	fff	r		BS-1	Turner	UK	1901
Linda Campbell	dr	sd	4	sv	f	c	H	BS-2	Moore	USA	1991

THE VARIETIES	COLOR	FORM	HARDINESS ZONE	VIGOR	FRAGRANCE	SEASON	SUITABILITY FOR HEDGING	DISEASE SUSCEPTIBILITY	BREEDER	ORIGIN	INTRODUCED
Magnifica	mr	sd	3	sv	fff	r	H	BS-0	Van Fleet	USA	1905
Marie Bugnet	w	d	2-3	sv	fff	r	H	BS-0	Bugnet	Canada	1963
Martin Frobisher	lp	d	3	v	fff	c	H	BS-0	Svejda	Canada	1968
Mary Manners	w	sd	4	v	fff	c	H	BS-1	Leicester Rose Co.	England	1970
Max Graf	dp	s	4	g	f	s		BS-0	Kordes	Germany	1919
Mme. Georges Bruant	w	sd	4	sv	fff	c	H	BS-0	Bruant	France	1887
Mrs. Anthony Waterer	dr	d	3	sv	f	c	H	BS-2	Waterer	UK	1898
Moje Hammarberg	m	d	3	v	fff	r	H	BS-0	Hammarberg	?	1931
Nova Zembla	w	d	5	v	fff	r	H	BS-1,R	Mees	UK	1907
Nyveldt's White	w	s	4	sv	fff	r	H	BS-1	Nyveldt	Holland	1955
Pierette Pavement	mp	sd	2-3	sv	fff	r	H	BS-0	Uhl	Germany	1987
Pink Grootendorst	mp	d	3-4	sv	f	c	H	BS-1	Grootendorst	Holland	1923
Pink Pavement	mp	sd	2-3	sv	fff	r	H	BS-0	Uhl	Germany	?
Polareis	w	sd	4	sv	ff	r	H	BS-1	?	?	?

COLOR
w=white or nearly white
p/w=pink and white
pb=pink blend
p/y=pink and yellow
lp=light pink
mp=medium pink
dp=deep pink
mr=medium red
dr=deep red
rb=red blend
m=mauve
mb=mauve blend
ly=light yellow
my=medium yellow
dy=deep yellow
yo=yellow-orange
o=orange
or=orange-red
yo=yellow-orange
c/s=coppery salmon

FORM
s=single
s+=slightly more than single
sd=semi-double
d=double
vd=very double or quartered

HARDINESS ZONE
2 to 5 (see Zone map)

VIGOR
g=ground cover
l=low
sv=semi-vigorous
v=vigorous
cl=climber

FRAGRANCE
f=little or no fragrance
ff=moderate fragrance
fff=exceptional fragrance

SEASON
sp=spring
s=summer
r=repeating
c=continuous bloomer

SUITABILITY FOR HEDGING
H

DISEASE SUSCEPTIBILITY
Blackspot:
BS-0= Immune or so little as to be insignificant.
BS-1= Noticeable but generally affecting fewer than 25% of leaves.
BS-2= Affecting at least 50% of leaves, some defoliation without protection.
BS-3= Affecting most of leaves, heavy defoliation without protection.

Mildew:
M=Varieties that are particularly susceptible to mildew.

Rust:
R= Varieties that are particularly susceptible to rust.

Note: Although roses are subject to several diseases, by far the most important disease of hardy varieties is blackspot. Those in drier climates may not have problems with blackspot, but in more humid areas blackspot can seriously affect many roses. These designations are based on the incidence of blackspot in a moderately humid site. Although you may find the incidence of blackspot either more or less severe than indicated by these ratings, they at least will offer a relative scale of blackspot susceptibility.

THE VARIETIES	COLOR	FORM	HARDINESS ZONE	VIGOR	FRAGRANCE	SEASON	SUITABILITY FOR HEDGING	DISEASE SUSCEPTIBILITY	BREEDER	ORIGIN	INTRODUCED
Pristine Pavement	w	sd	2-3	sv	fff	r	H	BS-0	Uhl	Germany	?
Purple Pavement	m	sd	2-3	sv	fff	r	H	BS-0	Uhl	Germany	?
Rosa paulii	w	s	2-3	g	fff	s		BS-0,M	Paul	UK	1903
Rose à Parfum de l'Hay	dr	d	4	sv	fff	c		BS-1	Gravereaux	France	1901
Roseraie de l'Hay	dr	sd	4	v	fff	c	H	BS-0	Cochet-Cochet	France	1901
Rugosa repens rosea (*Rosa × paulii rosea*)	lp	s	2-3	g	fff	s		BS-0	Paul	UK	1912
Ruskin	dr	d	3-4	v	fff	r	H	BS-1	Van Fleet	USA	1928
Sarah Van Fleet	mp	sd	4	sv	fff	c	H	BS-1,R	Van Fleet	USA	1926
Scabrosa	m	s	2-3	v	fff	c	H	BS-0	Harkness	UK	1960
Scarlet Pavement	dp	sd	2-3	sv	fff	r	H	BS-0	Uhl	Germany	?
Schneelicht	w	s	4	v	ff	r	H	BS-1	Geschwind	Hungary	1894
Schneezwerg (*Snow Dwarf*)	w	sd	2-3	sv	fff	c	H	BS-0	Lambert	Germany	1912
Sir Thomas Lipton	w	d	3-4	v	fff	c	H	BS-0	Van Fleet	USA	1900
Snow Pavement	w	sd	2-3	sv	fff	r	H	BS-0	Baum	Germany	1986
Souvenir de Philemon Cochet	w	d	2-3	v	fff	c	H	BS-0	Cochet-Cochet	France	1899
Thérèse Bugnet	mp	d	2	v	fff	r	H	BS-0,M	Bugnet	Canada	1950
Topaz Jewel	my	sd	5	sv	ff	r		BS-2	Moore	USA	1987
Vanguard	c/s	sd	5	v	fff	r	H	BS-1	Stevens	USA	1932
Wasagaming	mp	d	2-3	sv	ff	s		BS-1	Skinner	Canada	1938
White Grootendorst	w	d	3-4	sv	f	c		BS-1	Eddie	UK	1962
White Pavement	w	sd	2-3	sv	fff	r	H	BS-0	Uhl	Germany	?
Will Alderman	mp	d	2-3	sv	ff	c		BS-1	Skinner	Canada	1949

THE VARIETIES	COLOR	FORM	HARDINESS ZONE	VIGOR	FRAGRANCE	SEASON	SUITABILITY FOR HEDGING	DISEASE SUSCEPTIBILITY	BREEDER	ORIGIN	INTRODUCED
ROSA SETIGERA											
American Pillar	dp	s	5	cl	f	s		BS-0	Van Fleet	USA	1902
Baltimore Belle	lp	d	5	cl	f	s		BS-1	Feast	USA	1843
ROSA SPINOSISSIMA (ROSA PIMPINELLIFOLIA)											
Aïcha	my	s+	3	cl	ff	sp		BS-1	Petersen	Denmark	1966
Altaica	w	s	3	sv	f	sp	H	BS-0	Species	Asia	c. 1818
Dr. Merkeley	mp	d	3	l	fff	s		BS-1	Skinner	Canada	c. 1924
Doorenbos selection	rb	s	3	l	ff	r		BS-0	Doorenbos?	Germany?	?
Double pink (Burnet double pink)	mp	d	3	sv	fff	sp		BS-0	unknown	UK	c. 1800s
Double white (Burnet double white)	w	d	3	sv	fff	sp		BS-0	unknown	UK	c. 1800s
Double yellow (Old Yellow Scotch)	my	d	3	sv	ff	sp		BS-1	unknown	UK	c. 1800s

COLOR
w=white or nearly white
p/w=pink and white
pb=pink blend
p/y=pink and yellow
lp=light pink
mp=medium pink
dp=deep pink
mr=medium red
dr=deep red
rb=red blend
m=mauve
mb=mauve blend
ly=light yellow
my=medium yellow
dy=deep yellow
yo=yellow-orange
o=orange
or=orange-red
yo=yellow-orange
c/s=coppery salmon

FORM
s=single
s+=slightly more than single
sd=semi-double
d=double
vd=very double or quartered

HARDINESS ZONE
2 to 5 (see Zone map)

VIGOR
g=ground cover
l=low
sv=semi-vigorous
v=vigorous
cl=climber

FRAGRANCE
f=little or no fragrance
ff=moderate fragrance
fff=exceptional fragrance

SEASON
sp=spring
s=summer
r=repeating
c=continuous bloomer

SUITABILITY FOR HEDGING
H

DISEASE SUSCEPTIBILITY
Blackspot:
BS-0= Immune or so little as to be insignificant.
BS-1= Noticeable but generally affecting fewer than 25% of leaves.
BS-2= Affecting at least 50% of leaves, some defoliation without protection.
BS-3= Affecting most of leaves, heavy defoliation without protection.

Mildew:
M=Varieties that are particularly susceptible to mildew.

Rust:
R= Varieties that are particularly susceptible to rust.

Note: Although roses are subject to several diseases, by far the most important disease of hardy varieties is blackspot. Those in drier climates may not have problems with blackspot, but in more humid areas blackspot can seriously affect many roses. These designations are based on the incidence of blackspot in a moderately humid site. Although you may find the incidence of blackspot either more or less severe than indicated by these ratings, they at least will offer a relative scale of blackspot susceptibility.

THE VARIETIES	COLOR	FORM	HARDINESS ZONE	VIGOR	FRAGRANCE	SEASON	SUITABILITY FOR HEDGING	DISEASE SUSCEPTIBILITY	BREEDER	ORIGIN	INTRODUCED
Frühlingsanfang	w	s	4-5	v	fff	sp	H	BS-1	Kordes	Germany	1950
Frühlingsduft	ab	sd	4-5	v	fff	sp	H	BS-1	Kordes	Germany	1949
Frühlingsgold	my	s+	4-5	v	fff	sp	H	BS-2	Kordes	Germany	1937
Frühlingsmorgen	dp	s	4-5	v	fff	r	H	BS-1	Kordes	Germany	1942
Frühlingschnee	w	sd	4-5	v	ff	sp	H	BS-1	Kordes	Germany	1954
Frühlingstag	dy	sd	4-5	v	fff	sp	H	BS-1	Kordes	Germany	1949
Gloire de Edzell (*Glory of Edzell*)	mp	s	4	v	ff	sp	H	BS-1	unknown	unknown	?
Harison's Salmon	c/s	s	3	sv	ff	sp	H	BS-0	Hamblin	?	1929
Harison's Yellow (*Yellow Rose of Texas*), (*R. × Harisonii*)	my	sd	3	sv	f	sp	H	BS-1	Harison	USA	1830
Hazeldean	my	sd	2-3	sv	f	sp	H	BS-1	Wright	Canada	1948
Kakwa	lp	d	3	sv	fff	sp	H	BS-0	Wallace	Canada	1973
Karl Förster	w	sd	4-5	sv	fff	r		BS-0	Kordes	Germany	1953
Maigold	yo	sd	5	v	fff	s		BS-1	Kordes	Germany	1953
Mary Queen of Scots	mp	s	3	l	ff	sp		BS-1	unknown	UK?	?
Mrs. Colville	rb	s	3	sv	ff	sp		BS-1	unknown	UK?	?
Petite Pink Scotch	mp	s	3	g	ff	sp		BS-1	unknown	UK?	*c.* 1750
Single Cherry	mr	s	3	l	ff	sp		BS-1	unknown	UK?	?
Stanwell Perpetual	lp	d	3	sv	fff	c	H	BS-0	Lee	UK	1838
Suzanne	lp	vd	3	sv	f	c		BS-1	Skinner	Canada	1949
William III	mb	sd	3	l	fff	s		BS-1	unknown	UK?	?
ROSA SUFFULTA											
Assiniboine	dp	d	3	sv	ff	s		BS-1	Marshall	Canada	1962
Cuthbert Grant	dr	d	3-4	sv	f	c		BS-1	Marshall	Canada	1967

THE VARIETIES	COLOR	FORM	HARDINESS ZONE	VIGOR	FRAGRANCE	SEASON	SUITABILITY FOR HEDGING	DISEASE SUSCEPTIBILITY	BREEDER	ORIGIN	INTRODUCED
ROSA XANTHINA											
Canary Bird	dy	s	4-5	sv	f	sp		BS-1	?	?	1907
MISCELLANEOUS SHRUBS											
Adelaide Hoodless	dr	sd	4	l	f	r		BS-2	Marshall	Canada	1973
Alexander Mackenzie	mr	d	3-4	v	ff	c	H	BS-0	Svejda	Canada	1985
Birdie Blye	mp	d	4-5	sv	f	r	H	BS-1	Van Fleet	USA	1904
Bonica '82 (Bonica)	lp	d	5	l	f	c	H	BS-1	Meilland	France	1985
Captain Samuel Holland	lr	sd	3-4	v	f	r		BS-0	Agr. Canada	Canada	1990
Carefree Beauty (*Bucbi*), (*Audace*)	mp	sd	4	sv	f	r		BS-1	Buck	USA	1977
Champlain	dr	sd	4	l	f	c		BS-0	Svejda	Canada	1982
Constance Spry (*Constanze Spry*)	mp	d	4	v	fff	s		BS-0	Austin	UK	1961
Cuthbert Grant	dr	d	4	sv	ff	r		BS-2	Agr. Canada	Canada	1967
De Montarville	lr	sd	4	l	f	r		BS-0	Agr. Canada	Canada	1997
Dortmund	dr	s	5	cl	f	r		BS-1	Kordes	Germany	1955

COLOR
w=white or nearly white
p/w=pink and white
pb=pink blend
p/y=pink and yellow
lp=light pink
mp=medium pink
dp=deep pink
mr=medium red
dr=deep red
rb=red blend
m=mauve
mb=mauve blend
ly=light yellow
my=medium yellow
dy=deep yellow
yo=yellow-orange
o=orange
or=orange-red
yo=yellow-orange
c/s=coppery salmon

FORM
s=single
s+=slightly more than single
sd=semi-double
d=double
vd=very double or quartered

HARDINESS ZONE
2 to 5 (see Zone map)

VIGOR
g=ground cover
l=low
sv=semi-vigorous
v=vigorous
cl=climber

FRAGRANCE
f=little or no fragrance
ff=moderate fragrance
fff=exceptional fragrance

SEASON
sp=spring
s=summer
r=repeating
c=continuous bloomer

SUITABILITY FOR HEDGING
H

DISEASE SUSCEPTIBILITY
Blackspot:
BS-0= Immune or so little as to be insignificant.
BS-1= Noticeable but generally affecting fewer than 25% of leaves.
BS-2= Affecting at least 50% of leaves, some defoliation without protection.
BS-3= Affecting most of leaves, heavy defoliation without protection.

Mildew:
M=Varieties that are particularly susceptible to mildew.

Rust:
R= Varieties that are particularly susceptible to rust.

Note: Although roses are subject to several diseases, by far the most important disease of hardy varieties is blackspot. Those in drier climates may not have problems with blackspot, but in more humid areas blackspot can seriously affect many roses. These designations are based on the incidence of blackspot in a moderately humid site. Although you may find the incidence of blackspot either more or less severe than indicated by these ratings, they at least will offer a relative scale of blackspot susceptibility.

THE VARIETIES	COLOR	FORM	HARDINESS ZONE	VIGOR	FRAGRANCE	SEASON	SUITABILITY FOR HEDGING	DISEASE SUSCEPTIBILITY	BREEDER	ORIGIN	INTRODUCED
Dr. Merkeley	mp	d	2-3	l	ff	s	H	BS-0	unknown	Siberia int	1924
Flamingo	mp	sd	5	v	ff	r		BS-1	Howard	USA	1956
Frontenac	mp	sd	3-4	l	f	c	H	BS-0	Agr. Canada	Canada	1992
George Vancouver	lr	sd	3	sv	f	r	H	BS-0	Agr. Canada	Canada	1994
Golden Wings	my	s+	5	sv	ff	c		BS-2	Shepherd	USA	1956
Henry Kelsey	dr	sd	4	cl	ff	c		BS-1	Svejda	Canada	1984
Hope for Humanity	dr	d	3-4	l	f	r		BS-1	Agr. Canada	Canada	1995
John Cabot	mr	d	3	cl	f	c		BS-0	Svejda	Canada	1978
John Davis	mp	d	3	v	ff	c	H	BS-0	Svejda	Canada	1986
John Franklin	mr	sd	4-5	l	f	c		BS-2	Svejda	Canada	1980
J.H. Kern	m	vd	4	l	ff	c		BS-2	Kern?	USA?	?
J.P. Connell	my	d	3-4	sv	ff	r		BS-2	Svejda	Canada	1987
Lambert Closse	lp	d	4	l	ff	r		BS-1	Agr. Canada	Canada	1995
Leverkusen	my	sd	4-5	cl	ff	s	H	BS-0	Kordes	Germany	1954
Louis Jolliet	dp	d	3	v	f	c	H	BS-0	Agr. Canada	Canada	1990
Marie Bugnet	w	sd	3	v	fff	r	H	BS-1	Bugnet	Canada	1963
Marie Victoran	p/y	d	4	sv	ff	r		BS-1	Agr. Canada	Canada	1998
Morden Amorette	mr	d	3-4	l	f	c		BS-2	Marshall	Canada	1977
Morden Blush	w/lp	d	3	l	f	c		BS-2	Collicutt-Marshall	Canada	1988
Morden Cardinette	mr	d	3-4	l	f	c		BS-2	Marshall	Canada	1980
Morden Centennial	mp	d	3	sv	ff	r		BS-1	Marshall	Canada	1980
Morden Fireglow	or	sd	3	l	f	c		BS-2	Collicutt-Marshall	Canada	1989
Morden Ruby	dp	d	3	l	f	c		BS-2	Marshall	Canada	1977

THE VARIETIES	COLOR	FORM	HARDINESS ZONE	VIGOR	FRAGRANCE	SEASON	SUITABILITY FOR HEDGING	DISEASE SUSCEPTIBILITY	BREEDER	ORIGIN	INTRODUCED
Morden Snow Beauty	w	s+	3-4	l	f	r		BS-1	Agr. Canada	Canada	1999
Morden Sunrise	y	s+	3-4	l	f	r		BS-1	Agr. Canada	Canada	1999
Mrs. John McNabb	w	vd	3	sv	ff	r	H	BS-1	Skinner	Canada	1942
Nearly Wild	mp	s	3-4	l	f	c		BS-1	Brownell	USA	1941
Nicholas	dr	sd	4	l	f	r		BS-1	Agr. Canada	Canada	1996
Parkdirector Riggers	dr	s+	5	v	f	c		BS-1	Kordes	Germany	1957
Polstjärnan (*Polestar*), (*The Polar Star*), (*The Wasa Star*), (*The White Star of Finland*), (*Wasastjernan*)	w	s	3	cl	f	s		BS-0	Wasast-Jarnan	Finland	1937
Prairie Dawn	mp	d	3	v	f	s		BS-1	Agr. Canada	Canada	1959
Prairie Joy	mp	d	4	l	f	r	H	BS-2	Agr. Canada	Canada	1990
Quadra	dr	vd	4	v	f	r		BS-0	Agr. Canada	Canada	1994
Rheinaupark	dr	sd	5	sv	f	c		BS-2	Kordes	Germany	1983
Robusta	dr	s	4-5	v	f	c		BS-1	Kordes	Germany	1987
Rote Max Graf (*Red Max Graf*), (*Kormax*), (*Kordes' rose*)	dr	s	5	g	f	s		BS-0	Kordes	Germany	1980

COLOR
w=white or nearly white
p/w=pink and white
pb=pink blend
p/y=pink and yellow
lp=light pink
mp=medium pink
dp=deep pink
mr=medium red
dr=deep red
rb=red blend
m=mauve
mb=mauve blend
ly=light yellow
my=medium yellow
dy=deep yellow
yo=yellow-orange
o=orange
or=orange-red
yo=yellow-orange
c/s=coppery salmon

FORM
s=single
s+=slightly more than single
sd=semi-double
d=double
vd=very double or quartered

HARDINESS ZONE
2 to 5 (see Zone map)

VIGOR
g=ground cover
l=low
sv=semi-vigorous
v=vigorous
cl=climber

FRAGRANCE
f=little or no fragrance
ff=moderate fragrance
fff=exceptional fragrance

SEASON
sp=spring
s=summer
r=repeating
c=continuous bloomer

SUITABILITY FOR HEDGING
H

DISEASE SUSCEPTIBILITY
Blackspot:
BS-0= Immune or so little as to be insignificant.
BS-1= Noticeable but generally affecting fewer than 25% of leaves.
BS-2= Affecting at least 50% of leaves, some defoliation without protection.
BS-3= Affecting most of leaves, heavy defoliation without protection.

Mildew:
M=Varieties that are particularly susceptible to mildew.

Rust:
R= Varieties that are particularly susceptible to rust.

Note: Although roses are subject to several diseases, by far the most important disease of hardy varieties is blackspot. Those in drier climates may not have problems with blackspot, but in more humid areas blackspot can seriously affect many roses. These designations are based on the incidence of blackspot in a moderately humid site. Although you may find the incidence of blackspot either more or less severe than indicated by these ratings, they at least will offer a relative scale of blackspot susceptibility.

THE VARIETIES	COLOR	FORM	HARDINESS ZONE	VIGOR	FRAGRANCE	SEASON	SUITABILITY FOR HEDGING	DISEASE SUSCEPTIBILITY	BREEDER	ORIGIN	INTRODUCED
Royal Edward	mp	s+	4	l	f	r		BS-0	Agr. Canada	Canada	1995
Scharlachglut (*Scarlet glow*), (*Scarlet fire*)	dr	s	4-5	v	f	s		BS-1	Kordes	Germany	1952
Shropshire Lass	lp	s+	5	v	ff	s		BS-1	Austin	UK	1968
Simon Fraser	mp	s+	4	l	f	c	H	BS-0	Agr. Canada	Canada	1992
William Baffin	dp	s+	3	cl	f	c	H	BS-0	Svejda	Canada	1983
William Booth	mr	s	3	v	f	c		BS-0	Agr. Canada	Canada	1999
Windrush	ly	s+	4	sv	f	r		BS-2	Austin	UK	1985
Winnipeg Parks	dr	d	3	l	f	r	H	BS-2	Agr. Canada	Canada	1993
Zitronenfalter	my	sd	5	sv	ff	r		BS-2	Tantau	Germany	1956

APPENDIX
Nurseries, Rose Organizations and Source Books

NURSERIES

The following nurseries are known to carry hardy roses and are believed to ship plants. There are doubtless other nurseries that sell hardy roses and the inclusion of these nurseries is in no way an endorsement of their products.

The Antique Rose Emporium
Route 5, Box 143
Brenham, Texas 77833 USA
Telephone: 409-836-9051
Catalog: $2.00

Carl Pallek & Son Nurseries
Box 137
Virgil, Ontario L0S 1T0 Canada
Telephone: 416-468-7262
Free catalog, does not ship to USA

Carroll Gardens, Inc.
P.O. Box 310
Westminster, Maryland 21157 USA
Telephone: 301-848-5422
301-876-7336, outside Maryland
800-638-6334

Corn Hill Nursery Ltd.
RR 5, Route 890
Petitcodiac, N. B. E0A 2H0 Canada
Telephone: 506-756-3635
Catalog: $2.00

Country Bloomers Nursery
20091 East Chapman Ave.
Orange, California 92669 USA
Telephone: 714-633-7222

Earl May Seed & Nursery L.P.
Shenandoah, Iowa 51603 USA
Telephone: 800-831-4193

Forevergreen Farm
70 New Gloucester Road
North Yarmouth, Maine 04021 USA
Telephone: 207-829-5830
Free catalog

Greenmantle Nursery
3010 Ettersburg Road
Garberville, California 95440 USA
Telephone: 707-986-7504

Gurney Seed & Nursery
110 Capitol Street
Yankton, South Dakota 57079 USA
Telephone: 605-665-4451

Heritage Rosarium
211 Haviland Mill Road
Brookeville, Maryland 20833 USA
Telephone: 301-774-2806
Catalog: $1.00

Heritage Rose Gardens
16831 Mitchell Creek Drive
Fort Bragg, California 95437 USA
Telephone: 707-964-3748,
707-984-6959

Heritage Rose Group
c/o Miriam Wilkins
925 Galvin Drive
El Cerrito, California 94530 USA
Telephone: 415-526-6960

High Country Rosarium
1717 Downing at Park Avenue
Denver, Colorado 80218 USA
Telephone: 303-832-4026

Historical Roses
1657 West jackson Street
Painesville, Ohio 44077 USA
Telephone: 216-357-7270

Hortico, Inc.
Robson Raod, RR 1
Waterdown, Ontario L0R 2H1 Canada
Telephone: 416-689-6984
Catalog: $2.00

Inter-State Nurseries
P.O. Box 10
Louisiana, Missouri 633353-0010
USA
Telephone: 314-754-4525
800-325-4180

Jackson & Perkins Co.
2518 South Pacific Highway P.O. Box 1028
Medford, Oregon 97501 USA
Telephone: 503-776-2000
800-872-7673 (customer service)
800-292-4769 (to place orders)

Kimbrew-Walter Roses
Route 2, Box 172
Grand Saline, Texas 75140
Telephone: 214-829-2968

Krider Nurseries
P.O. Box 29
Middlebury, Indiana 46540 USA
Telephone: 219-825-5714

Lowe's Own Root Roses
6 Sheffield Road
Nashua, New Hampshire 03062 USA
Telephone: 603-888-2214
Catalog: $2.00

Morden Nurseries Ltd.
P.O. Box 1270
Morden, Manitoba R0G 1J0 Canada
Telephone: 204-822-3311

Park Seed Company, Inc.
Cokesbury Road
Greenwood, South Carolina
29647-0001 USA
Telephone: 803-223-8555
800-845-3369 (out of state)
800-922-6232 (within south Carolina)

Pickering Nurseries Inc.
670 Kingston Road, Hwy. 2
Pickering, Ontario L1V 1A2 Canada
Telephone: 416-839-2111
Catalog: $2.00, price list free

Roseberry Gardens
Box 933, Postal Station F
Thunder Bay, Ontario P7C 4X8
Canada
$100.00 minimum order

Roses by Walter LeMire
Highway 3 & Oldcastle Road North
RR 1, Old Castle, Ontario,
N0R 1L0 Canada

Roses of Yesterday & Today
802 Brown's Valley Road
Watsonville, Califonia 95076 USA
Telephone: 408-724-3537
Catalog: $3.00
Sears McConnell Nurseries

Port Burwell, Ontario
N0J 1T0 Canada

Sheridan Nurseries Ltd.
1116 Winston Churchill Boulevard
Oakville, Ontario L6J 4Z2 Canada

V. Krauss Nurseries Ltd.
Carlisle, Ontario L0R 1H0 Canada
Telephone: 416-689-4022

Wayside Gardens
1 Garden Lane
P.O. Box 1
Hodges, South Carolina
29695-0001 USA
Telephone: 800-845-1124

ROSE ORGANIZATIONS

The American Rose Society
P.O. Box 30,000
Shreveport, Louisiana 71130 USA
Membership: $32.00 ($23.00 for
those over age 65)

The Canadian Rose Society
Anne Graber
10 Fairfax Crescent
Scarborough, Ontario M1L 1Z8
Canada
Telephone: 416-757-8809
Membership: $25.00, $27.00 for
family

The Royal Rose Society
The Secretary
Chiswell Green
St. Albans, Hertfordshire
England AL2 3NR
Telephone: (0727) 50461

SOURCE BOOKS

There have been innumerable books
written on roses. It would be fruitless
to list them all as many are out of
print, while others have little information on the hardy roses. The following
books are valuable for those seeking
more information on hardy roses.

Beales, Peter, Classic Roses, Holt,
Rinehart and Winston, New York,
1985

Beales, Peter, Twentieth Century
Roses, Harper & Row Publishers, New
York, 1988

Cairns, Thomas, ed. Modern Roses
10, American Rose Society; (List of all
registered roses and roses of historical
or botanical importance), 1993

Dobson, Beverly, Combined Rose List,
Beverly R. Dobson, 215 Harriman
Road, Irvington, New York 10533,
USA (A list of all rose varieties avail-
able in commerce.)

Griffiths, Trevor, The Book of Classic
Old Roses, Penguin Books, USA, 1988

Griffiths, Trevor, The Book of Old
Roses, Penguin Books, USA, 1987

Krussman, G., Roses, Batsford,
London, 1982 and Timber Press,
Portland, 1981

Taylor, Norman, Taylor's Guide to
Old-Fashioned Roses; (Taylor's Pocket
Guides to Gardening series), 1989

Taylor, Norman, Taylor's Guide to
Roses; (Taylor's Pocket Guides to
Gardening series), 1986

Thomas, G. S., Shrub Roses of Today,
J. M. Dent & Sons, 1974

Thomas, G. S., The Old Shrub Roses,
J. M. Dent & Sons, 1978

INDEX